for much closer scrutiny by the people of Presidential candidates to determine their fitness to govern a democratic nation in a democratic way.

The Accountability of Power draws on the author's own experiences both as a Senator and Presidential candidate. It analyzes the current structure of Presidential campaigns; the explosive growth of White House staffs and resources and their effects on our President; the decline and limited renaissance of Congress as a co-equal branch of government; the importance of the Nixon impeachment proceedings; and the impact of Presidential dealings with the media and the political parties. In each area, Senator Mondale offers cogent suggestions on changes that could introduce new vitality into the relationship between Presidents and other key institutions.

The Accountability of Power emphasizes the continuing need for strength in the Presidency, but insists that this strength must be matched by an equal emphasis on openness and responsiveness by our Chief Executives. Senator Mondale makes clear that another Vietnam or Watergate could occur again unless we rethink our attitudes toward the Presidency and insist upon absolute Presidential respect for the law.

Senator Mondale is the senior Senator from Minnesota. He was born in Ceylon, Minnesota, and earned his B.A. and law degrees from the University of Minnesota. He served as Attorney-General of Minnesota from 1960 through 1964, when he was appointed to the Senate to fill the unexpired term of the newly elected Vice President, Hubert H. Humphrey. He won election to the Senate in 1966 and was re-elected in 1972. He has become a leading figure on Capitol Hill during recent years, though he is still in his 40s. This is his first book.

The
Accountability
of
Power

The Accountability of Power

Toward a Responsible Presidency

by

Senator

WALTER F. MONDALE

David McKay Company, Inc.
New York

Library of Congress Cataloging in Publication Data
Mondale, Walter F, 1928-
    The accountability of power: ⁵⁵·

    Includes index.
    1. Presidents—United States. 2. Executive Power—
United States. I. Title.
JK516.M62 353.03 75-30907
ISBN 0-679-50558-X

MANUFACTURED IN THE UNITED STATES OF AMERICA

To Joan, Teddy, Eleanor Jane, and William

Foreword

This book represents my effort to describe what I believe the Congress, other institutions and we as Americans must do to protect our system and our liberties from the encroachment of an unaccountable Presidency.

I came to the U.S. Senate on the last day of 1964, and brought with me from Minnesota the then generally accepted view that we had to rely greatly on the President of the United States and on his judgment. I believed that our country had vast responsibilities and tremendous power to influence world events—and that we needed to influence those events in a way that squared with our view of what the world should be.

When President Kennedy called for virtually unlimited involvement in world affairs in his 1961 inaugural address, I had been thrilled along with most Americans. Most of us generally believed then in the importance of a very strong Chief Executive, in the need to rely on his judgment, as well as the judgments of his key advisors and agencies. This mood still prevailed when Lyndon Johnson and Hubert Humphrey were elected in 1964 by what was then the largest margin in American history. And it was reflected in the public opinion polls, which showed that both the new President and the Congress were enormously popular. The war, while heating up, was of less importance to the people than the domestic concerns on which we concentrated, almost exclusively, in the early part of the 89th Congress.

The country was optimistic about the future, about our dominant place in the world, and about our ability to deal with our problems at home and abroad. We felt confident that we had the resources to solve those problems.

Then things began to change. We escalated the war in Vietnam dramatically, and the number of American dead rose accordingly. Budgets for the Great Society programs froze. Doubts arose and grew about the massive deployment of naval, army and air forces in Southeast Asia. In four short years the party that had been elected with such broad public support was turned out of the White House. Richard Nixon was the new President, but despite his promises the war continued, and without our knowledge, other wars were underway in Cambodia and in Laos. American optimism was disappearing rapidly. The sense of humanity and helpfulness that underlay the Great Society was already gone, having been destroyed by the war and by a new national strategy to create suspicion, division and a sense of selfishness in the American people.

We did not know it then, but another trend was under way

that would constitute the worst and most pervasive political scandal in American history. It was a scandal so pernicious and so profound as to have threatened our very system of constitutional representative government.

While Vietnam and Watergate are very different issues, I am convinced that, particularly for my generation of political leaders, both raise fundamental questions about trends that took shape in the last decade and led to what Arthur Schlesinger, Jr., called the "Imperial Presidency." If we have learned nothing else in the last ten years, we now know the consequences of having a President who is largely unaccountable to Congress, to the law or to the American people. But we also know that without a stronger Congress, vigorous media and viable political parties the chances of keeping Presidents accountable are greatly diminished.

The "Imperial Presidency" may be in decline now because our Vietnam policy failed and because of the profound public reaction that nearly led to the impeachment of President Nixon. But I believe that we must analyze what forces produced it, what the dangers were and still are, and what steps must be taken to prevent the recurrence of another decade such as we've been through. This kind of analysis must be made lest Vietnam and Watergate fade in our memories without our having learned their painful lessons.

Both Vietnam and Watergate contained exceedingly dangerous implications for the future. While most Americans were quite aware of the war's essential elements, they nevertheless believed that the United States had vast ability to influence the course of events around the world.

Many of us, and I regret to include myself, also believed that our President and the agencies advising him not only were privy to vast amounts of classified information that better enabled them to know what was wise, best and practical, but also, because of their experience and ability, that they were better qualified to reconcile doubts concerning their policies. We know now, through the Pentagon Papers and other documentation, that great divisions and doubts existed within the executive and the Defense Department—doubts that were identical to those being expressed publicly by reporters, war experts and others both in Vietnam and here at home. We also know that the President and others used deceit, misrepresentation, excessive secrecy and other manipulative practices to cause the nation to persevere despite its growing doubts.

We were unaware of these abuses at the time, but we could see the tremendous influence of the executive and its ability to pressure and manipulate American society, together with its strong tendency to insulate itself from community concerns, and even from reality itself. We also witnessed the executive disclination to consider other reasonable options—as the case in Vietnam—and then to "circle the wagons" against comment and criticism and doubt. Lyndon Johnson described it as "hunkering down."

Watergate showed the ultimate and most profound usurpation of power by a President in American history. No matter how illegal or deceitful the options, all of them apparently were explored. Agencies such as the FBI, the Justice Department, the CIA and the IRS were used to intimidate political opposition. Efforts were even made to undermine the judicial system through perjury, attempted bribes of potential witnesses and an improper offer to a sitting judge.

All of this came against a background of a decade in which the Congress had often abdicated its responsibilities and handed over great amounts of power to our Presidents. Congress's war powers, our power of the purse, our confirmation power and our general power of oversight and investigation all seemed to be in danger of succumbing to a lack of congressional courage and an excess of faith in the omniscience of our Presidents.

I often had doubts that our representative system of government would survive. We might continue the system of electing a Congress and a President, I often thought, but would the Congress retain its power and responsibility under the Constitution as a coequal branch of government? And, for the first time, I experienced what happens to American society when the traditional powers of the Congress are disregarded, not asserted—or both.

The President's strategy of impounding appropriated funds, for example, showed his open disregard for the constitutionally mandated congressional power over the purse. To understand the devastating results of this strategy one must understand what it means to be a congressman.

Surely one of the basic functions in the Congress is to

assert the will of our state and constituents in the law-making processes of government. We are experts on our own states and districts. We spend our lives meeting and knowing our constituents, seeing and listening to their problems. We love our states, and, in my case, after nearly a quarter of a century of intensive public participation, I know Minnesotans and they know me. They rightfully demand attention to their problems, whether a late spring flood drowns the crops in western Minnesota or a steel plant closes in Duluth or dairy imports are flooding domestic markets or whatever. Minnesotans expect me to listen and respond to the needs of our state.

Because other senators and members of the House perform the same job for their states, legislation, appropriations and administative practices are made to conform with realities as our constituents see them. This molding of national objectives into state and local needs is an utterly indispensable function for a vital democracy. There is no other way of doing it. Not even the smartest bureaucrats could know, experience or be motivated enough to deal with the millions of separate problems in a nation of our size. And yet the Nixon administration believed it could—that it could undermine the representative function. Congress passed laws and appropriated funds to meet the people's needs as mandated by law, but that entire function was being undercut by Presidential government. Minnesotans would ask for more public housing for our senior citizens, and we would pass legislation to provide it. The legislation would be signed into law, and then nothing would happen. We would pass a law to provide assistance for farmers whose crops were destroyed in western Minnesota. It would be signed and then not enforced. Other members of Congress faced the same problem, and we began to get the sick feeling that our functions under the Constitution had been destroyed.

Despite all of these experiences, I came away basically optimistic for several reasons. First, in reaction to both the war and Watergate, the public showed great vision, wisdom and independence. It saw the folly of Vietnam before many of its leaders. It demanded a change in the course of that war even while its leaders were claiming that victory was still possible. Similarly, the public saw the enormity and dangers of Watergate despite massive efforts to conceal it. They saw through the lies and understood that this was not just another political scandal.

My optimism also has flowed from an increased admiration for and belief in the fundamental wisdom and strength of our Constitution. That wonderful document has withstood the stresses and strains of the last decade, not the least of which was an attempt to subvert and diminish its clear distribution of powers and fundamental prerogatives within our federal system. Fortunately, it proved much stronger than a powerful President who shrewdly, cynically and deceitfully tried to subvert it. And it revealed again the wisdom of its makers, whose understanding of human nature proved as relevant and appropriate to the restraint of tyranny in the 1970s as it did two hundred years ago.

The needs expressed in the Constitution for accountable public officials and for full public disclosure have proven the best guarantees of American liberty. I believe that my generation of public officers has a special responsibility to carefully probe and analyze the anatomy of the devastation through which we have passed in the last decade and to concentrate on the constitutional problems that have been exposed.

I do not want a weak President. The President of the United States living within the constitutional law well may be the strongest public officer in the world. The resources at his command are staggering. His ability to communicate with the American people—on his own terms—is overwhelming because of the instant communication provided by radio and television. The budgets he controls are massive. His authority over appointments and nominations in the executive branch and the judiciary, his ability to veto legislation not to his liking, and his control over foreign policy all give him fantastic power. But he must act within the constitutional parameters of that power. And he must be in continual contact with other institutions such as the Congress, the media and the parties that are themselves vigorous and capable of constantly reminding him of the limitations of the law and the role of public opinion. If all this occurs and if he serves with full appreciation and affection and respect for the American people, he can even become the moral, almost spiritual, leader of our country.

The legitimate strengths of the President make it terribly important that he be accountable to the American people and not be limited by his personal appraisal of his own stewardship. He must give the American people the facts and advise them of policy alternatives so that they can judge him according to their standards and desires. Our Presidents must tell the truth and they must obey the law. If they behave in this fashion, our country will remain healthy and secure.

I want that to happen because I have spent the last ten years in the United States Senate suffering along with all Americans through a war that may have been this nation's greatest mistake and through a scandal that could have destroyed America.

That is why I wrote this book. And I only hope that my attempt to analyze what went wrong and to suggest what must be done to prevent it from ever happening again will be of some value.

Acknowledgments

I am deeply indebted to Roger Colloff, a gifted legislative assistant on my Senate staff, who more than anyone else provided the impetus behind this book. Beginning early in 1973 and continuing through the impeachment summer of 1974, he provided invaluable help to my legislative efforts to bring a higher degree of accountability to a runaway Presidency, efforts which ultimately led to a major speech on the subject delivered in the Senate in the fall of 1973 entitled "The Presidency and Watergate: An Agenda for Reform." The speech in turn persuaded us to broaden our efforts further by undertaking this book. Throughout its preparation Roger gave tirelessly and generously of his time and talents. I cannot imagine the project without him.

I am also indebted to Richard Moe, my Administrative Assistant, whose adult career has been dedicated to making our political process and political party system work effectively. His suggestions have been exceedingly helpful.

I am grateful to a number of perceptive students of the Presidency who graciously shared with me their wisdom and experience and who were kind enough to react to early drafts with suggestions that were invariably helpful. Primary among these are Joseph Califano, Jr., Thomas Cronin, Congressman Donald M. Fraser, Harry McPherson, Jr., Richard Neustadt, and Arthur Schlesinger, Jr.

My sincere thanks and admiration go to James O'Shea Wade, whose persistence, patience, and pluck helped greatly to get this project under way, and to Truman M. Talley, whose consummate professionalism and good judgment helped see it through to completion. Not least, I am indebted to Ernest Lotito, whose skillful editing of the manuscript made it infinitely more readable, and to James Johnson, whose encouragement and help were more than generous.

September 8, 1975
Washington, D.C.

WALTER F. MONDALE

Contents

1

The Presidency
in Crisis

The President of the United States is a man or a woman or whatever who is, like, picked by the people to lead the country. And they try to make the person almost perfect . . . because if a person is going to be the head of a country like the United States for four years, he just has to just about be perfect.
— *Twelve-year-old boy, interviewed by Fred Greenstein, 1970*

I never questioned anything. I grew up during World War II and honestly thought that God was on our side, but I won't be so naïve again and neither will my children. I have a four-year-old who watches the hearings and keeps asking if they are going to put the President in jail.
— *Mother of five, Westchester County, N. Y.,*
interviewed in August 1973

Security guard Frank Wills could not have known it at the time, but on June 17, 1972, he helped end an age of innocence for Americans. His discovery of a strip of tape on a door in a plush Washington office building known as Watergate led to disclosures of wrongdoing beyond anything that Americans had believed their Presidents were capable of undertaking. Watergate—and all it came to represent and

1

symbolize—forced Americans to focus on the nature of the Presidency, which had been fashioned over history, and on the personalities of the Presidents who had held that office.

Since the Presidency of Franklin Roosevelt, Americans had become accustomed to the idea of a growing and ever more powerful Presidency at the head of a growing and ever more powerful federal government. Americans looked to their Presidents for moral leadership, a sense of direction in the formulation of public policy, and statesmanship in protecting America from continuing threats—real or imagined—from overseas. Roosevelt had transformed both the expectations of the people toward their Presidents and the nature of the Presidential establishment itself. Fostered by a world war and then by the cold war, the development of nuclear weapons and by the needs of a growing nation at home, Americans had become accustomed to the idea of Presidential leadership on a scale never before exhibited in the history of our republic.

The pull of a powerful Presidency became a dynamic relationship between those occupying the office and the institution itself. Those whose personalities welcomed greater Presidential power encouraged the development of an aggressive Presidency. And even those who began with limited conceptions of the role of the Presidency often came to accept a broader view of Presidential power.

Dwight Eisenhower came to office in 1953 desiring a limited Presidential role. Under Harry Truman, a yearly, detailed Presidential legislative package had been developed, which had greatly changed the relationship between Congress and the Presidency in the President's symbolic role in the formulation of legislative programs for the nation. But Eisenhower in 1953 refrained from submitting a Presidential legislative program. The criticism was massive and the result was predictable. In 1954, he presented a package of his own containing some sixty-five proposals for new legislation. As Richard Neustadt has noted, "Throughout, one theme was emphasized: here was a comprehensive and coordinated inventory of the nation's current legislative needs reflecting the President's own judgments, choices and priorities in every major area of Federal action." Thus Eisenhower was forced by public demand to take the initiative in proposing a comprehensive legislative package.

That much of this legislative package was never adopted —indeed, was never seriously pursued by Eisenhower— misses the point. The pressures of the Roosevelt legacy had impelled Eisenhower, an essentially passive successor, into the position of providing symbolic leadership. Americans expected their Presidents to provide this kind of leadership; and while some Presidents were pushed, most eagerly responded to and indeed helped create and encourage this view of the Presidency. Indeed, this view of the Presidency as the preeminent source of national power and wisdom acquired ever-increasing strength throughout most of the 1960s. Surrounded by weak institutions and encouraged by a public perception of the Presidency as the only institution capable of moving an often sluggish government, the escalation of Presidential power proceeded nearly unchecked.

Within a few years, this inflated sense of Presidential power, so dangerous in the long run to our democracy, tripped over Vietnam and fell over Watergate. By the late 1960s, with America engaged in a seemingly endless and unwinnable land war in Asia, the people's confidence in their governmental institutions—and inevitably in the Presidency—had begun to erode. And just as Americans' perception of the inflated sense of the Presidential role had distorted reality, so the fall from grace was distorted and magnified as well.

If Vietnam burst the bubble of Presidential ascendency and omniscience, Watergate began a wholesale decline in Americans' belief in the viability and honesty of their governmental institutions. The measures of this disillusionment are many, and they are frightening. In 1960, 63.1 percent of the nation's electorate voted in the Presidential election; by 1972, the figure was down to 55.6 percent. In a technique developed and used in eighteen countries by Cantril and Free to measure individuals' faith in their nation's achievements, the United States in 1971 became only the second nation—the Philippines in 1959 was the first—to judge that its present condition was worse than it had been five years before.

The decline in Americans' faith in all key institutions in the late 1960s and early 1970s, as measured by pollster Louis Harris, was astounding. In 1966, 41 percent of the nation had confidence in the executive branch of the government; by 1973, the figure was down to 19 percent. Congress, the Supreme Court, business and labor were also not spared from this declining sense of confidence in our institutions. In just one year—from 1972 to 1973—the ravages of Watergate on the people's faith in the institution of the Presidency became evident. The University of Michigan Institute of Social Science Research found that while in 1972, 41.4 percent of those questioned felt that the President was the branch of the government most often trusted to do what was right, by 1973 the figure was down to 23.7 percent. Significantly, the same survey indicated that slightly more of those questioned in 1973 felt that the Presidency was the most powerful institution in government—35.3 percent, as opposed to 33.6 percent in 1972. The American people seemed to realize that the Presidency was powerful, indeed, that it was the most powerful institution in our governmental apparatus. And yet Americans profoundly doubted whether this power was being used properly—whether the Presidency was a vehicle for the achievement of proper goals through proper means.

Fundamental questions were being asked about the Presidency, both by those who had supported and by those who had opposed the expansion of Presidential power. These questions posed a fundamental challenge to the strength of our governmental institutions.

While Americans in the early 1970s had serious cause to wonder about the acceptable boundaries of Presidential power, they certainly were not the first to ponder the problem. Indeed, no question had more absorbed the group of talented revolutionaries meeting in 1787 to hammer out the form of government for our new American nation. They were deeply wary of the accumulation of power in any one institution of government, a fear fostered by the tyrannical abuse of power under the King of England and by the inept mismanagement by state legislatures during the Confederation. Perhaps the classic statement of this fear—and of the solution for it—was Madison's comment in Federalist Paper No. 51:

> To what expedient, then, shall we finally resort, for maintaining in practice the necessary partition of power among the several departments, as laid down in the Constitution? . . . In order to lay a due foundation for that separate and distinct exercise of the different powers of government, which to a certain extent is admitted on all hands to be essential to the preservation of liberty, it is evident that each department should have a will of its own. . . . The great security against a gradual concentration of the several powers in the same

6

department, consists in giving to those who administer each department the necessary constitutional means and personal motives to resist encroachments of the others. . . . Ambition must be made to counteract ambition.

Basically, the framers decided that human nature was such that the occupants of public office must be subject to clear restraints. If a public institution permits unrestrained accumulations of power, they reasoned, the holder of that power might act in ways entirely inconsistent with the needs of the public, the nation and the law. And it was therefore considered necessary to divide power, to check it, and to require those who exercised that power to explain its use and give the American public a basic veto power in the form of recurrent elections which could be conducted with a full understanding of the interplay and tension between the branches of government. And this tension would help ensure that when disputes arose between the branches of government they would be forced into public view, so that the people would have the ability to sway the recalcitrant branch. By so transforming intragovernmental disputes into public matters for discussion, the Constitution helped ensure public participation in the governing process.

The danger was not conceived to lie in a particular branch of government, but rather in the potential for the concentration of excessive power in any branch. The fear was not of the exercise of power, but of the exercise of unaccountable power. And the solution was not the deprivation of power from the federal government, but the separation of powers which would make that power accountable. The questions Americans were asking in the late twentieth century were almost precisely those expressed in Philadelphia nearly two hundred years earlier.

Had the power of the executive so outstripped the power of the other competing institutions in our government that there remained no means of restraining the arbitrary use of that power? And who was going to restrain the exercise of unaccountable power, if it was to be restrained at all? Indeed, for many—including many previously committed supporters of the concept of expanding Presidential power—the answers to those questions seemed to determine whether our democratic institutions would survive the shocks they had suffered. Jefferson had warned that "the tyranny of the legislature is really the danger most to be feared and will continue to be so for many years to come. The tyranny of the executive power will come in its turn but at a more distant period." His warning now seemed to have been realized, and the Presidency had been thrown into crisis.

This crisis had been the result of an accumulation of power begun first and most noticeably in foreign affairs. As Arthur Schlesinger, Jr., observed, "The Imperial Presidency was essentially the creation of foreign policy."

For many years, a bipartisan coalition with a broad ideological base chose to overlook the ever-increasing ability of the Presidency to dominate those other institutions inside and outside government that might act as restraints on the unaccountable use of power in international dealings.

In 1944, Justice Jackson observed in the *Korematsu* case that "The chief restraint upon those who command the physical forces of the country in the future as in the past must be their responsibility to the political judgments of their contemporaries and to the moral judgments of history." Unfortunately, by the middle 1960s, many of the institutions capable of rendering that political judgment had atrophied so badly that only the moral judgments of history were acting as restraints on Presidential power.

Institutions which had traditionally shared power—most notably, Congress and the political parties—seemed to have broken down as effective checks. A bipartisan foreign policy which had dominated so much of the post–World War II era had contributed to this breakdown. By necessity or choice, foreign policy had become the chief means for exercising Presidential power. De Tocqueville's prediction had been fulfilled: "If the existence of the union were perpetually threatened, if its chief interest were in daily connection with those of other powerful nations, the executive government would assume increased importance in proportion to the measures expected of it and to those which it would execute."

Presidents discovered that foreign policy had many advantages for a leader seeking to avoid true accountability. It can be intoxicating. The sweep and drama of diplomatic initiatives, the need for only limited consultation, the tendency of Americans to rally behind Presidents in international efforts during times of crisis, and the frequent absence of powerful opposing interest groups, so often preent in domestic affairs, enabled them to maintain secrecy and avoid real power-sharing.

Recent Presidents have concentrated heavily on foreign affairs. A number of White House aides of recent administrations, interviewed by political scientist Thomas E. Cronin, estimated that the Presidents for whom they worked spent between 60 percent and two-thirds of their time exclusively concentrating on national security activities or foreign policy crises. For Richard Nixon this seemed to come naturally, as his interests lay in the area of foreign policy. But the lure of foreign involvement consumed even Lyndon Johnson, with his deep commitment to domestic improvement. His dreams for a more just and humane America were smothered in the jungles of Vietnam where over 55,000 American lives and $150 billion in American treasure were lost.

Yet the tragedy of Vietnam was not the tragedy of Presidents alone. Vietnam was a trauma begun in a spirit of American omnipotence, a spirit that we could solve the world's problems and reshape much of the world in our own image. Only painfully did we learn the limits of American power. Together we suffered as our blood and resources were fruitlessly squandered in Southeast Asia. We came to see the Presidency no longer as the source of omniscience supported by the Pentagon's computers, but as an office occupied by mere mortals who could make serious mistakes. We came to see the need for a Congress which challenged and questioned executive leadership and asserted its powers under the laws and the Constitution.

Then, just as the end of direct American military involvement in Vietnam concluded one national nightmare, we began another. The use of secrecy and national security to justify any action had been transferred from the foreign policy arena and used against the American people. As the late Stewart Alsop observed: "to transfer such secret service techniques on an obviously planned and organized basis to the internal American political process is a genuinely terrifying innovation. The Watergate scandal, it is clear, by now, is different—truly different, different in kind—from all the scandals that have preceded it in American history. It is this difference that makes it so frightening."

This "difference" meant use of the IRS, the CIA, the FBI and the Department of Justice for corrupt ends designed to subvert the political process and punish the enemies of the Nixon Presidency. The "difference" meant deceit, perjury and the cover-up of unlawful activity involving the President of the United States. It meant a full-scale attempt to destroy the integrity of the election process itself through the use of secret agents, the exaction of large corporate contributions from major American companies with the expectation of government favors, and the use of some of the funds so raised to seek to destroy the credibility of honorable men seeking the nomination for President of the United States.

The catalog of Watergate horrors is seemingly endless. We could have lost our democracy. The Presidential mentality which bred Watergate also led to the illegal impoundment of huge sums of congressionally appropriated funds to frustrate policy objectives adopted by the Congress; a campaign of media harassment and intimidation beyond anything seen before; and the rejection by the President of the role of his own political party in any meaningful way during the election of 1972. It bred contempt for the American people and our institutions and shattered the trust of the American people.

How had this all happened? How had the American people, the Congress, the parties, the media, indeed virtually all our American institutions permitted these tragedies to occur? That American involvement in the war in Vietnam was ended, that Watergate was discovered and dealt with effectively by these same institutions should give us some comfort. Yet the inability of these institutions to check arbitrary Presidential behavior at the outset must be fully explored and understood. For unless we deal effectively with the causes of these Presidential excesses, we may well see them happen again. And we can prevent Presidential excess without fundamentally weakening the much-needed power of the Presidency.

To learn from the ordeals of Vietnam and Watergate, however, we must analyze carefully their similarities and differences. Both Vietnam and Watergate have helped change Americans' view of their Presidents and the Presidency. Americans have awakened to the need for institutional change if such tragedies are to be avoided in the future. Yet each—while reflecting in part the high price we pay for unaccountable Presidential conduct—occurred in a different environment, and from each we must learn important lessons.

The disastrous consequences of American involvement in the Vietnamese War destroyed both the notion of American omnipotence and the concept of Presidential omniscience. It was the product of a belief in Presidential authority and competence in the area of foreign affairs accumulated over two decades. Following World War II and the Korean War, following the "loss" of China and the spread of communism in Eastern Europe, we became increasingly willing to defer to Presidents, to assume that Presidents knew, or could know, all the facts and knew how best to deal with them.

There was deception by Presidents Johnson and Nixon concerning their Vietnam policies. Both concealed from the American people their true intentions and plans regarding Vietnam. In April of 1965, when the first large-scale escala-

13

tion of the war occurred with the introduction of 20,000 troops into Vietnam, a top advisor to the President wrote in an internal and secret memorandum that "the President desires that premature publicity be avoided by all possible precautions. The actions themselves should be taken as rapidly as practicable but in ways that should minimize the appearance of sudden changes in policy. The President's desire is that these movements and changes should be understood as being gradual and wholly consistent with existing policy." Following closely on the heels of the Gulf of Tonkin resolution—approved by the Congress on the basis of dubious information—this policy of secrecy was continued throughout the prosecution of the war in Vietnam.

In 1968, the people narrowly chose Richard Nixon to be President on the basis of his promises to bring the war to an end. Less than one year later, secret bombing raids in Cambodia began, and more than 100,000 tons of bombs were dropped in 3,500 sorties. In fact, Pentagon figures show about 3 million tons of bombs were dropped in Indochina during the first three years of the Nixon Presidency, more than had been dropped during the three final years of Lyndon Johnson's Presidency. Along with the secret bombings came a continued expansion of the war into other areas of Indochina and the loss of over 15,000 American lives in the years 1969 through 1972.

It is true that Congress may have been provided misleading information to justify the Gulf of Tonkin resolution. And it is true that the Pentagon Papers reveal a Presidential strategy at odds with what the Congress and the American people were being told. But the unavoidable fact is that the main outline and realities of the war in Vietnam were obvious for all to see. The war in Vietnam was the best-reported war in American history. Whatever deception may have been attempted, the American people—and the Congress—were able to see the destruction of innocent lives, the burning of villages, the entire gamut of physical and psychological warfare from the comfort of their easy chairs. We in the Congress knew what we were doing when we regularly voted continuing appropriations for American troop involvement in Vietnam. The American people knew what tens of billions of their tax dollars were paying for each year.

We knew, and yet for too long we were willing to pay the price. We knew what was happening, but we somehow thought we could win, that we could "tough it out." We didn't and we couldn't, and as a society we paid a high price. Vietnam's costs went beyond even its terrible toll in lives and money. It provoked a confrontation between generations and poisoned American politics. It was a tragedy caused by the nearly unquestioned dominance of Presidential assertions of power in foreign affairs, the weakness of congressional dissent, and the illusion—widely shared by Americans —of the limitless nature of American power, resources and wisdom.

Watergate was fundamentally different, and yet shared

many common elements of Presidential excess. The war in Vietnam was knowable to everyone; Watergate was not, at least at first. The tragedy of Watergate was not a tragedy of American miscalculation, led by a vision of Presidential power which had outgrown reality. Rather, in its broadest scope, it was the tragedy of men who fundamentally lacked respect for the system of American values which governed our history and used the weakness of many other governmental institutions as an excuse to attempt to change the nature of those institutions.

The men of the Nixon White House were not responding to a public which seemed eager to attempt to imprint American involvement in a foreign nation. They were instead responding to their own vision of a society in which individual freedoms were cheapened, in which the powers of the Congress were systematically disregarded, in which the parties were ignored, and in which the media were treated as objects for intimidation. And yet the weakness of the institutions surrounding these men must have played a part in giving them the sense of security needed to undertake the massive violations of law that they undertook.

Vietnam and Watergate were fundamentally different in their origins, in their development, and in their effects on our society. Yet both showed the complex interplay between Presidential personality, institutional strength and public opinion which marks our politics.

The personality of Lyndon Johnson was clearly important

in the escalation of the war in Vietnam and the imprint it left on American society. Yet he inherited involvement in the war from other Presidents, and was encouraged in his escalations by an American public which wanted American involvement and a Congress basically responding to that desire. Without public support, there might have been less congressional willingness to go along with American policy. With a strong Congress able to help lead public opinion, we might have shown the American public earlier the tragic consequences of our Vietnam involvement. With a different Presidential personality, there might have been less of a desire to attempt to show America's ability to police the world. But if the public had been more strongly opposed to the war, even Johnson or Nixon might have relented far earlier than they did.

So, too, the mixture of personality, institutions and public opinion is complex even with Watergate. With a man different from Richard Nixon—without his distrust of the media, of the Congress, of the parties and even of the constitutional system—Watergate probably never would have occurred. Yet even with Nixon, had there been a vigorous Congress checking many of the early excesses of his administration, he might have been restrained in his unaccountable assertions of power.

Even with Richard Nixon in office, had the American public reacted more strongly and swiftly after Watergate disclosures began to be known in mid-1972, the grievous damage done to our country in the year and a half before the President resigned might have been lessened. An earlier Presidential resignation would have accomplished much.

Again, the blend of personality, institutions and public opinion is inseparable. The challenge we face, therefore, in the wake of Vietnam and Watergate is complex.

We must elect Presidents who respect the law and the other institutions which surround the Presidency. We must strengthen those institutions in ways which increase their effectiveness and their ability to check unaccountable Presidential power. And as Americans we must be aware of the importance of a restrained yet strong Presidency, of the need for Presidents who respect the need for accountability while asserting the valid powers of their office, and of the need for a Congress, parties and media which can and will check otherwise unaccountable Presidential conduct.

The task we face is clear: to redefine the role of the Presidency to acknowledge the importance of Presidential power, but to insist on the greater importance of accountable Presidential power. The "end of innocence" of the American people with their Presidents can turn out to be a healthy development by allowing us all to see, as Lord Acton saw, that "there is no worse heresy than that the office sanctifies the holder of it."

This restraint can be accomplished only through the reform of the institutional relationships between our Presidents and other bodies in our society and by changing the ways that Americans examine the character and personality of those persons who wish to lead the nation. We must see that both the reform of institutions and the changes in the way we look at Presidential character must be more than passing phenomena. We cannot forget Watergate and Vietnam, and we cannot allow the resignation of a President to end our search for ways to avoid their repetition.

Since Gerald Ford has become President, our memories of Vietnam and Watergate have faded. The "Imperial Presidency," we are told, is a creature of the past, unlikely to be repeated. Without doubt, the Ford personality is far more open and accountable than is Richard Nixon's. Without doubt, the Congress has continued to reassert its institutional prerogatives under President Ford, though not always as vigorously as many of us would hope. Without doubt, President Ford has used the Cabinet more than many of his predecessors and in most instances has been fair in his dealings with the media.

Gerald Ford has once again proven the powerful influence of a President's personality on that office. Ironically, though he was not elected, Gerald Ford has shown the enormous value of electing Presidents who are healthy emotionally. Yet even he granted an unconditional pardon to Richard Nixon, an act taken with little consultation and very little perception of the public reaction to its enormous significance.

Presidential personality giveth and Presidential personality can taketh away. And we should therefore not assume that our problems with Presidential overreachings can be solved if we only have the right person in the office.

Those who believe that we need only elect "good people" and that the institutions and public awareness will take care of themselves overlook the damage to our institutions which another prolonged period of institutional neglect could ensure. In our satisfaction over the presence in the White House of an individual who seems to have a healthy personality, we cannot forget the need to continue the institutional changes begun in recent years. In our relief that the law is once again being respected by our President, we cannot forget the dangers of an unrestrained and unaccountable Presidency.

We can neither completely "Watergate-proof" nor "Vietnam-proof" our Presidency. But we *can* attempt to construct new institutional relationships that reduce the possibility of Presidential illegality. We *can* attempt to ensure closer scrutiny of the personality and character of our Presidents so that the likelihood of another Richard Nixon becoming President is lessened. Most importantly of all, we can seek through all these means to restrain the exercise of unaccountable power so that the wisdom of the American experiment is once again given new meaning.

Many public and private institutions must be strengthened. The Congress should employ its wide powers over a broad range of domestic and international affairs as an active force in helping shape American government; it should not merely react to Presidential uses of that governmental apparatus. The Cabinet's role as Presidential advisors should not preclude the exercise by Cabinet officers of creative leadership of the departments whose functions they oversee. The role of the political parties is crucial to restrain runaway Presidents and to focus and channel the feelings of Americans about their government. The media's importance in forcing Presidents to face reality cannot overshadow their responsibility to serve as vehicles for expression of a wide variety of ideas in areas relating not only to government but also to a broad scope of human concerns.

Yet the ability of each of these institutions to now serve as restraints on Presidential lack of accountability acquires an importance unequaled in nearly two hundred years of democratic government. The tests and upheavals of the past decade dictate that each be given greater strength, not to reduce legitimate Presidential power as retribution for past excesses but to reduce unaccountable Presidential power as a protection for our democracy.

We will require strength in our Presidency, but no President in the future should be able to use that strength to weaken our system of government. The risks of not acting now are great. As Richard Neustadt observed just before the resignation of Richard Nixon:

> We are now in a period of anti-political politics with journalists and politicians playing to their own sense of

successive, cumulative, public disillusionments. Watergate feeds the mood. When such a period descended upon us in the early 50's, we got Eisenhower for President, the hero above politics. Since we lack heroes nowadays, the next time could be worse. Moreover, the renewed constraints on Nixon cannot last forever. Watergate's effects will wear off over time, perhaps by his successor's second term, taking us no further than 1984. As this occurs, the weakened state of old constraints would be exposed once more. The parties gone beyond recall, the Congress mortgaged to ticket splitting, the cabinet frayed by overlapping jurisdictions, the dependence of all the rest on the President's own style.

This is a somber prediction, as frightening now as when it was first offered. It need not come to pass. It must not if our democracy is to survive the increasing strains to which it will be subjected. And it will not if we insist that the tragedies of recent years are given a redeeming value through the lessons they teach us as we begin the third century of our democracy.

2

The Road to
the White House

The Presidency is not a prize to be won by mere glittering promises. It is not a commodity to be sold by high pressure salesmanship and national advertising. The Presidency is a most sacred trust and it ought not to be dealt with on any level other than an appeal to reason and humanity.

—*Franklin D. Roosevelt*

I'm not an old experienced hand at politics. But I am now seasoned enough to have learned that the hardest thing about any political campaign is how to win without proving that you are unworthy of winning.

—*Adlai Stevenson, 1956*

One of the most popular lines circulating in political Washington during 1975 was that the Democrats would be a sure thing to recapture the White House in 1976 if only they didn't have to nominate a Presidential candidate. Unfortunately for the Democrats, no one has yet come up with a way of getting around that necessity, and, if the experiences of 1968 and 1972 are of any value, it may again prove to be a chief obstacle in their effort to defeat the Republicans in November. For reasons that few claim to fully understand, there seems to be something inherent in the nominating process which has given the Democratic Party an uncanny but increasingly dependable way of snatching defeat from the jaws of victory.

Regrettably, this is only one of many serious problems with the way in which we select Presidential candidates. It is indisputably one of the most important processes in our entire political system, but it is also one of the most irrational. It has evolved over nearly two hundred years without design, structure or purpose into a complex maze of state laws, party regulations and unwritten traditions. No other major nation chooses its leaders in such a chaotic manner, and the question is whether we should continue to do so.

In one of their few serious oversights, the Founding Fathers believed that political parties would not and *should* not play a role in the American political system. They provided instead that every four years the states would choose electors who, being acknowledged leaders in their communities and therefore learned in such matters, would wisely select the most qualified man to be President of the United States. It took less than a decade for the much-feared "factions" to appear, however, and not much longer for political parties to weave themselves forever into the political fabric of the new republic.

After experimenting with congressional caucuses to select their Presidential nominees, the parties soon adopted the uniquely American institution of the national nominating convention to do the job, and they have been at the heart of the process ever since. Parties have come and gone, but the conventions have remained; the major changes in the last century have had almost exclusively to do with the manner in which the convention delegates were chosen.

Since delegates to national conventions would select the Presidential nominee, their own selection was obviously the pivotal point of the process. The states opted for a wide variety of delegate selection procedures, some choosing precinct caucuses and state conventions, others choosing some kind of popular primary, and still others choosing some combination of these systems; no two states were—or are —exactly alike. Only seldom was it seriously argued that the Presidential nomination process was a *national* process that deserved a *national* design. It was viewed instead as a matter to be left exclusively to the states; to this day, neither the Congress nor the parties themselves have believed they could or should play more than a strictly secondary role in the process.

There are some who believe that there is an accidental genius inherent in our present chaotic nominating process, that it provides a process of natural political selection which eliminates lesser candidates and which permits the more able and durable to survive. There may be something to this notion, but not much.

It is a point usually made by those whose candidates have done well by the process, and has thus crept into our political mythology. My own view is that it's often a mindless process from the candidates' perspective, too often a self-defeating one for the parties, and frequently an ineffective one for the nation. A *New York Times* editorial summed it up this way:

> It is fatuous to describe as participatory democracy a nominating system that involves a wretchedly small proportion of the electorate, that in some states encourages Democrats to help choose Republican candidates and vice versa, that grossly distorts the significance of the first few primary contests in an election year and rewards with money and inordinate publicity the states that hold them. It is a system that, as now constituted, allows candidates to run in states where they expect to do well and avoid those where they can't, that turns the whole process into a contest for psychological momentum and that subjects a Presidential hopeful to a crazy quilt of conflicting rules, forbidding costs and a physically staggering campaign schedule.

I have been amazed at how little thoughtful discussion and analysis has been devoted to the process of running for the Presidency. It is a process, after all, at the very core of our governmental system, and yet there is an inexplicable absence of sophisticated literature on the way we encourage or discourage Presidential candidates, on the burdens we impose upon them and the hurdles we erect in the path of their nomination and election, and on the relevance of these and other factors to the kind of Presidents we ultimately elect.

From early 1973 until November 1974, I actively sought the Democratic Presidential nomination and in the process concluded that the manner in which we nominate and elect Presidential candidates is badly in need of fundamental review.

The process of seeking the Presidency almost defies description, particularly for someone like myself who was seeking the office for the first time, who was largely unknown outside of my own state and region, and who was of ordinary financial means. It is a process which involves assembling an experienced and qualified core staff, raising funds in staggering quantities, and traveling to every corner of the nation in preparation for a series of delegate selection systems each of which is unique. It involves an inordinate period of time, commencing now almost four years before the election, and it increasingly consumes a larger portion of each day. It involves an unending effort to become more widely known through speeches, TV and radio appearances, newspaper interviews, public and private conferences with party and other leaders, all in addition to a full legislative agenda in the Senate. It involves time away from one's family, one's job, and rest. It involves a fatigue and a resulting danger to one's perspective which, if allowed to go unchecked, poses serious potential problems for the candidate's outlook and approach. It involves all of this and more, most of which I never fully appreciated before I experienced it.

I want to emphasize that I do not believe the White House should be easily achieved by anyone. It should be a difficult process. Candidates should be forced to go through fire in order to win the Presidency. They should be required to campaign intensively in every part of the country and to answer all kinds of questions in order to learn what is on people's minds and to respect differing regions and differing points of view. It is a learning process unlike any other. One cannot help but learn of the infinite diversity of our great country as well as its vastness and scope. One meets literally thousands of people, the powerful and those without power, each of whom has a right to be heard and respected in the assertion of his or her point of view. I am convinced that there is no other way of developing the understanding, sensitivity and respect essential to responsible leadership which even approximates the value of a Presidential campaign.

In his book *Decision Making in the White House,* Ted Sorensen related John Kennedy's experiences through a long and grueling campaign for both the nomination and the November election. Sorensen concluded during the campaign that the physical burdens imposed on a candidate were wholly unnecessary and indeed were counterproductive to his being a good President. After serving in the White House, however, he decided that those talents and skills which were most essential to an effective campaigner and which were refined through years of constant use—the ability to persuade, the need to assimilate facts quickly, the ability to resolve disputes and to act decisively under pressure—were the same talents and skills needed in the Presidency.

I fully agree with Sorensen's conclusion, but I believe at the same time that the entire process needs profound and fresh analysis which will result in making it more nearly fitted to human scale. When I announced on November 21, 1974, that I was withdrawing from the Presidential race, I did so on the grounds that I simply did not have the overwhelming desire to do what was necessary in order to be nominated and elected, that I loved my work in the Senate and my close ties to Minnesota and that to continue the campaign would seriously interfere with both. It was a difficult political decision, made even harder by my belief that I was making substantial progress, but in the end it was a fairly simple personal one because it reflected my own priorities.

I was amazed, however, at some of the reactions. Much of my mail and comments from friends suggested that what my decision really meant was that a normally healthy person could not persevere and overcome the tremendous burdens imposed on Presidential candidates under our system, that the system itself screened out persons with sound mental health, leaving us with candidates so single-mindedly obsessed with the pursuit of the Presidency that they were willing to disregard the normal and necessary aspects of a healthy life. We were in the process of producing a Presidency, many believed, that would only be occupied by a distorted and unstable personality. Richard Nixon had resigned the Presidency only three months earlier, and no doubt this experience reinforced this view in some minds. Nonetheless, it is a view which I reject.

I believe it is possible for people who love politics, who love the excitement and demands of a Presidential campaign, to be not only healthy but to benefit enormously from the learning process it affords and the other challenges it presents. The people a candidate encounters are usually helpful, understanding and supportive. Their appreciation of what the candidate is going through often renews his strength and determination to continue. Their thoughtfulness and support are constant aids to his sense of balance and perspective. At least all of this was a part of my own experience. I am convinced nevertheless that the system itself is becoming increasingly irrational, self-defeating and destructive of the ultimate goal of electing the most important political leader in a free society in the world.

There were several problems which became painfully apparent to me during the course of my campaign, one of which was the matter of life-style. My family life increasingly consisted of a long-distance phone call late at night. I traveled some 200,000 miles through more than thirty states, delivered hundreds of speeches and appeared on almost as many radio and TV programs, shook thousands of hands and held countless meetings and conversations. For the most part, I enjoyed much of this activity, but the days became increasingly longer, often up to eighteen hours, and they seldom permitted time for reading or for reflection. I can recall more than once becoming so tired that in the process of trying to read a newspaper I suddenly realized that I hadn't absorbed a single word that I had read. I remember trying to work on position papers or speeches when my fatigue simply wouldn't allow me to concentrate properly on them.

I love to ponder ideas, to reflect on them and discuss them with experts and friends over a period of time, but this was no longer possible. It struck me as being unfortunate and even tragic that the process of seeking the Presidency too often prevents one from focusing on the issues and insights and one's ability to express them, which are crucially important. I believe this fact explains many of the second-rate statements and much of the irrational posturing that are frequently associated with Presidential campaigns. In any case, after eighteen months I decided this wasn't for me. It wasn't my style and I wasn't going to pretend that it was. Instead of controlling events in my life, I was more and more controlled by them. Others have had an easier time adapting to this process than I did, and I admire them for it. But one former candidate told me, three years after his campaign had ended, that he *still* hadn't fully recovered emotionally or physically from the ordeal.

Related to this factor is the responsibility a candidate must feel to the public position he currently holds. Most Presidential candidates tend to be governors, senators, or representatives, and each one who holds such an office must inevitably ask himself whether he wishes to forsake, for all practical purposes, the public trust to which he has been elected in order to seek the Presidency. It can be a wrenching internal tug of war—at least it was in my case. Obviously the Presidency is the most important office in the nation and it is possible to justify a decision to devote less time to one's other duties on that ground alone. But I was increasingly troubled by the amount of time I was spending away from the U.S. Senate and away from Minnesota, to which I owe a great deal and for which I have great affection. By the fall of 1974 I was at the point where I had to decide between my responsibility to them on the one hand and to my Presidential race on the other. I knew I couldn't have it both ways any longer. If I was to continue my campaign, both it and my work in the Senate would inevitably suffer. This is a selection process which each candidate must sooner or later go through and which each must resolve in his own way.

One of the greatest difficulties confronting a new Presidential candidate, and often an insurmountable one, is the enormous problem of becoming known. There is no other effort to which a candidate and his staff devote a greater part of their time and energy, and there is no other effort which in the end usually frustrates them more. Only rarely do we develop Presidential candidates who are not already well known. Between 1936, when he first started taking such polls, and 1972, George Gallup found that only 62 Democrats and 47 Republicans attracted the support of at least *1 percent* of their party's voters. In my own case, the polls showed that by the time I withdrew some 40 percent of the public could identify my name but little else about me, and only 4 percent indicated support. Washington comedian Mark Russell liked to say that most people believed Mondale was a suburb of Los Angeles, and I think he was right.

No one really knows just how much television, radio and newspaper coverage is needed to become known in this vast nation of ours, but it is a lot. One can achieve wide recognition in one of two ways: through luck—including inheritance—or through months, or more probably years, of unremitting, bone-numbing speeches, interviews and other public appearances of all kinds. Although the latter course is the only one available to most candidates, it is also the less successful of the two. It is a course which increasingly requires longer and longer campaigns, more and more money, and the inevitable question of whether one's other responsibilities can be set aside to the extent necessary.

A look at the list of names most often mentioned for the Presidency in 1976 in public surveys underscores this observation. They are usually Americans of great distinction who have spent much of their political careers seeking the Presidency, or they have had some fortuitous event thrust them into national prominence and thus into Presidential consideration. For example, Gerald Ford was little known nationally despite twenty-five years in the House of Representatives, until he was named Vice-President; after becoming President, of course, he became the dominant national political figure overnight. Less dramatically, some of the senators who served on the Watergate Committee and who thereby received daily national TV coverage were elevated from unknowns to celebrities within a few months. But most of the others who have gained wide recognition are usually in their late fifties or sixties, and their recognition has come only after a lifetime in politics and several attempts at national office. By virtue of being a Vice-Presidential candidate in 1968 and then having sought the Presidency in 1972, Senator Edmund Muskie of Maine is clearly sufficiently known to be considered seriously. Governor George Wallace of Alabama is in his fourth White House attempt and, of course, he too is widely known. My friend and colleague Hubert Humphrey, who I think stands as an example of someone who has maintained a healthy attitude after seeking the Presidency several times, is almost always near the top of the recognition polls. Similarly on the Republican side, the polls show that most people only know such figures as Nelson Rockefeller, Ronald Reagan and Barry Goldwater, each of whom has figured prominently in past Presidential elections; other potential candidates are far back in the pack.

It is true that several candidates have achieved their party's nominations even though they were not widely known when they first launched their campaigns. Wendell Willkie, Adlai Stevenson, Barry Goldwater and most recently George McGovern all come to mind. But each of them also lost to his opposition in November. The fact is that since Warren G. Harding's election in 1920 (and perhaps in part because of it?), no candidate has been elected President who was not already widely known and accepted by a solid majority of the American people *at the time of his nomination.*

Those potential candidates who consistently do well in the recognition polls are frequently fine public leaders who deserve to be considered seriously for the Presidency. But it is a great tragedy, in my view, that serious consideration should be limited to these few. There are hundreds of gifted men and women in this country, many of whom would make superb Presidents, who also deserve consideration but who will never receive it because they are virtually unknown. I believe we pay a tremendous national price by denying ourselves the opportunity to renew the quality and nature of our potential leadership as a result of this fact.

Some unknown candidates attempt to overcome the recognition problem by taking strong positions on controversial issues designed to attract broad public attention, even though the position may not be well thought out or soundly based. This kind of high-risk strategy can prove to be embarrassing in the long run, however, and it is often self-defeating. Moreover, the spectacle of candidates jockeying for position with ever-escalating political rhetoric diminishes public respect for the Presidential election process as well as for politics generally.

Bridging the gap between known and unknown candidates presents one of the most serious problems of the nominating process, and I am afriad there are no easy answers to it. I have discussed it frequently with newspaper editors and leaders in the broadcasting industry, and I regret that only seldom have I felt that they appreciate the depth of the difficulty. The national political media usually follow the "star system" of giving primary coverage to those who are already well known. It is perhaps understandable that they should do so since they are competing with one another for the same listening, viewing or reading audiences. Why should they jeopardize their own competitive positions by covering someone who may or may not amount to something and who in any case is a subject of low public interest? And with a good deal of validity they also say their job is to follow the news, not to develop new national leadership.

It's hard to argue with that conclusion, but it's also exceedingly frustrating to go through the process of trying to become known in order to be taken seriously. During the time I was seeking the nomination I was on the TV network evening news programs no more than five or ten times. Twice I was fortunate enough to be on Sunday interview shows, and occasionally in a television documentary. The political press treated me fairly and in some cases generously. But even with that kind of coverage, it was clear as I traveled around that I had not broken through to the point where I was known by any substantial portion of the American people. And of those who did know me, I'm afraid not many knew much about who I was or what I stood for. It may be that this failure was largely the result of my own inability to make more news in such a way that attracted public attention and support, and if so, I'm prepared to accept that. But there are too many others, no doubt abler candidates than myself, who have had similar experiences with similar results for there not to be a discernible pattern. The net effect of that pattern is that unknown candidates for the Presidency must do little else than seek public recognition on an all-out basis for several years if they hope to be taken seriously by the time of the primaries. It is deeply unfortunate that this must be so, and it is even more unfortunate than there may be no clear remedy for it.

If attempting to become known is a candidate's most frustrating exercise, raising the money to finance that effort is surely the most distasteful. I absolutely hated it. Soliciting funds from those in a position to contribute is an expected but nonetheless onerous and time-consuming aspect of campaigning. Most of the people I talked to were pleasant, delightful persons who asked for and expected nothing in return for their contributions, but the number of hours spent in this pursuit was a major drain on my time. It is a strange commentary on American political campaigns that so much of a candidate's time is spent with well-to-do prospective contributors and so little with unemployed or disabled workers, welfare mothers, hard-pressed retirees, school children with learning difficulties, citizens concerned with the environment or others in similar positions.

There is no question but that a candidate must necessarily spend more time pursuing dollars for his campaign than he does pursuing policies for his Presidency. It's not that a candidate willingly chooses that set of priorities, but the system forces him to do so. I believe most candidates share my intense dislike for that fact, but they have no other choice if they hope to be successful. As we will see, public financing of elections has improved this situation somewhat, but not to the extent that many believe.

A more important problem was the traditional manner in which Presidential campaigns had been financed in America, which was, it is now commonly agreed, a national disgrace. Big money was needed to make the campaigns effective, and therefore big money was solicited. Whereas the general election campaigns of 1960 cost both parties $25 million, the figure was up to $60 million by 1972. And it is still climbing. Most Presidential candidates could not hope to raise this kind of money in small amounts from persons who simply wanted to help the cause of good government, and most of them—with the exception of George McGovern in 1972—never made the attempt. Instead, the traditional practice was to raise funds from almost anyone willing to contribute, regardless of his motives. Unfortunately, too often those willing to contribute large sums were not wholly disinterested in the actions of the federal government as they affected the contributor's own private interests.

It was a compromising and often corrupting system which I believe has contributed as much as anything in recent years to the lessening of public confidence in American government. But no one knew how potentially rotten the system really was until Watergate began to unfold in early 1973 and the *modus operandi* of Nixon's chief fund-raiser, Maurice Stans, became clear. The laundering of corporate funds, the sale of ambassadorships, the intimidation of firms doing business with or regulated by the federal government—all these and more have become familiar stories emerging from the most shameful chapter in American political history.

In a revealing portrait, a Nixon re-election campaign official in 1972 described to correspondent Frank Wright of the *Minneapolis Tribune* how Stans' system worked.

Maury gave us his three rules that he always worked by.

Number one, know your man and to what extent he can give. He would always research what problems a company had with the government, know them inside out. It is sort of terrifying when a solicitor that you're talking to knows the fact that you have problems, and it looks like he is looking at your soul.

Number two, name your amount before he can name his. . . .

Number three, Maury said you must say what is in it for the contributor not to have the Democratic guy in as president. . . . He would describe a contribution as an "insurance premium against McGovern." The premium was all figured out. If a guy had $1 million net worth, he would give $10,000. On a scale of $50 million, he should give $50,000. And $100 million, $250,000.

Perhaps no incident dramatizes the use of this system as well as the case of American Airlines. Herbert Kalmbach, one of President Nixon's principal fund-raisers, approached American board chairman George Spater at a time when American had pending before the Civil Aeronautics Board a plan for merger with Western Airlines, and indicated that a contribution of $100,000 was expected. As Spater recalled it, "I knew Mr. Kalmbach to be both the President's personal counsel and counsel for our major competitor [United Airlines]" and he concluded that "a substantial response was called for." That substantial response amounted to a total American Airlines contribution of $75,000 to the Nixon campaign, of which $55,000 was in illegal corporate funds.

Dramatically but tragically, the 1972 Nixon campaign showed just how compromising and potentially corrupting our traditional manner of financing Presidential campaigns really was.

Added to this is the absolutely incredible present system of state Presidential primaries and conventions. Candidates are confronted really with fifty different systems, each reflecting local biases and traditions and each unrelated to any comprehensible overall purpose or design. There is no rational basis for the schedule of primaries, for their timing, for the relationship of one to another, nor for the different statutory rules governing them. To complicate matters even more, the system is in a continual state of flux. States are forever either modifying or fundamentally overhauling their delegate-selection processes. In the last decade alone the number of states employing primaries has more than doubled; in 1976 more than thirty states, including virtually all of the large ones, will offer them, and they will select nearly 80 percent of the 1976 national delegates. As Ed Muskie's campaign discovered in 1972, it is impossible for any candidate to enter all of the primaries and hope to survive. Yet the proliferation of primaries even since 1972, resulting as it has from individual state decisions, completely ignores this basic fact and further exacerbates the underlying problem.

There is also the question of how representative primaries, as they now exist, really are. Is New Hampshire really a social, economic and political microcosm of the nation? No

41

one very seriously argues that it is, and yet New Hampshire casts an inordinate influence on the nominating process every four years simply because it holds the first primary. To a lesser degree the same point can be made about Florida and a number of other states. Every four years, it seems, several states engage in a frantic and unseemly competition to see whose primary will be first, only to have the competition resolved by the New Hampshire Legislature meeting in emergency session to protect its favored position. New Hampshire is a wonderful state and I always enjoyed campaigning there, but no single state is sufficiently representative of the rest of the nation to warrant its playing such a large and disproportionate role in the nomination process. The basic questions are whether state boosterism and other equally irrelevant factors should continue to determine primary schedules, and whether there might not be a more rational *national* approach to the problem.

There is also the inexcusable phenomenon of crossover voting, whereby some states permit Republicans to participate in Democratic primaries and vice versa. Although concentrated primarily in the Midwest as a remaining vestige of the progressive era, there is no more perfidious element in our political system. The *New York Times,* relying on Daniel Yankelovich's polling services, estimated that as many as half of George Wallace's votes in the 1972 Wisconsin Democratic primary may have come from Republicans. It's hard to imagine how a political party's nominating process could be more distorted by any other single device.

Despite the dramatic growth in the number of primaries, there are many states that still permit the selection of national delegates through individual participation in a combination of precinct caucuses and county, district and state conventions. This is the system we have had in Minnesota for many years and which, all things considered, has worked very well. It is one of the healthiest elements in our entire political process because it permits greater and more direct individual participation than any other system. If the current trend toward primaries continues, however, the Minnesota system may become an endangered political species.

Unfortunately, both the number and complexity of the rules imposed on these convention states by the Democratic Party are staggering. They are often also unfathomable. These rules largely accomplished their stated purpose of bringing greater openness and fairness to state delegate-selection processes that badly needed both, but they have also regrettably prompted many states to opt for the relative simplicity of primaries and thereby have hastened that unfortunate trend. As a result, the traditional blend of primary and convention states is becoming seriously out of balance.

All of this together—all of these disparate and unrelated elements which make up our present nominating system—raises serious and fundamental questions about the manner in which we select our national leaders, questions which troubled me throughout my own short-lived attempt at the Presidency and which I have thought about frequently ever since. The need to raise money, to participate in vastly different kinds of primaries and convention processes, to become widely known, to forsake one's family, one's friends and one's public responsibilities, to keep moving fifteen or eighteen hours a day without adequate rest or preparation, to do all of these things and more over a period of two or three years—they *must* raise questions about the kind of candidates the system attracts and about the kind of results it produces.

My perspective, of course, is that of a former candidate, and that must be a factor in evaluating what I have to say on the matter. But I don't believe that fact by itself precludes objectivity, because when I withdrew from the race I did so without disappointment or regrets. On the contrary, the experience was an invaluable one, and I am enormously glad that I went through it. I met and came to know literally hundreds of kind and thoughtful people throughout the country, many of whom generously supported me with their time, energies and resources. I believe I gained some insights into the vastness, the excitement and the strengths of this nation that I could have gained in no other way. I came to see even more than before the basic goodness that exists in American life and the way that people are genuinely concerned about our country and where it is headed. I became

44

more and more convinced of their intelligence and their goodwill.

It is a magnificent and wonderful country, and those who seek to lead it have a duty to learn about it and to respect it. They also have a duty to show the American people who they are and how they are structured emotionally and intellectually, to show the strength of their leadership as well as their policies. There is no escaping this process nor should there be, but somehow it must be reconciled with the need to make the system more rational and more closely scaled to human capabilities.

It may be that my own campaign experience was unique, in which case all of this should be dismissed forthwith. I don't believe that it was, however. Many times I have discussed these problems with Senate colleagues and others who also have sought the Presidency, and invariably they have agreed with most of the points I have tried to raise here. They agree particularly that there must be a way in which a candidate's time, intelligence and spirit can be better used to learn, to understand and to persuade others under circumstances that permit these processes to receive real emphasis during the campaign. The common theme of all those with whom I talked was that we must either move the system in this direction or further encourage development of a nominating process adverse to the best interests of the Presidency and the nation as a whole.

There have been some serious and well-intentioned attempts to reform the nominating process in recent years, but they have usually been patchwork efforts and they have often brought with them side effects which were never intended. The most fundamental and far reaching of these has dealt with how we finance our Presidential candidates.

Disclosures of the Nixon campaign shakedown lists and other elements of its 1972 fund-raising scandals prompted the Congress in 1974 to adopt a comprehensive system of public financing for future Presidential elections. The premise was very simple: allow candidates to run for the Presidency by relying on public funds rather than special interests so that, once elected, they would be unencumbered by even implied commitments to the latter. By using the dollar check-off provided on individual income tax forms, the Congress declared that, henceforth, the nominees of the two major parties would each be given approximately $22 million in federal funds for their general election campaigns; if they accepted these funds they could accept no private contributions. And in any case, they could spend no more than $22 million.

The congressional remedy for financing Presidential candidates during the preconvention period was more complex, but it too was directed toward eliminating the corrosive influence of large private contributions. The Congress adopted a variation of a plan originally introduced in the

Senate by Senator Richard Schweiker of Pennsylvania and myself which includes two basic elements: a limitation of $1,000 on the amount that any individual can contribute to a Presidential candidate, and a matching system of private and public contributions. The latter works as follows: Once a candidate for his party's nomination raises $5,000 in amounts of $250 and less in each of 20 different states, he qualifies for matching funds from the federal Treasury. For every private contribution of $250 or less, he is then entitled to a similar contribution in the form of public funds. There is a spending ceiling of $10 million in the preconvention period, up to half of which may be in the form of matching public funds.

Although we won't know how well this system works until after 1976, there is little doubt that it will go a long way toward freeing our Presidential candidates from the kind of compromising influences which have too often characterized past elections. It is, in my judgment, the most important single reform to emerge from the Watergate scandals. And it is my fervent hope that this new system will restore the integrity of the Presidential nominating process and thereby restore the confidence of the American people in that process as well as in the Presidency itself.

As significant as I believe this reform is, it would be short-sighted to believe that it will solve all of the system's problems overnight or that it won't have other effects which were neither anticipated nor intended. For example, the

47

need to raise the threshold money required to qualify for public funds means that most Presidential campaigns will begin earlier than ever before, this at a time when most people believe that campaigns are too long already. The undeniable fact, however, is that the raising of large amounts of money in very small contributions, particularly through direct-mail solicitation, requires a huge lead time. As a result, it will be the rule rather than the exception for Presidential candidates to begin their active campaigns two or three years before the nominating conventions. Also, the limitation on the size of private contributions appears to have made it more difficult rather than easier for unknown candidates to raise sufficient funds to get serious campaigns under way. Finally, the same limitation seems to have given a distinct advantage to those candidates whose campaigns are premised on emotionally charged or "high intensity" issues.

The experience of 1976 will doubtless tell us more about these side effects. Even if they materialize, however, their combined effect probably will not outweigh the restoration of public confidence in a nominating process too often compromised in the past by the reliance on private-interest money. But they do serve to illustrate how a well-intentioned reform effort can often have unforeseen results.

The parties as well as the Congress have attempted in recent years to correct obvious inadequacies in the nomination process. But the results of these efforts are mixed at best. Since the disastrous 1968 convention in Chicago, the Democrats have been particularly active in attempting to open up and democratize their nominating procedures. They largely succeeded in this effort, but in the process they persuaded many people in 1972 that they had established "quotas" for minority groups, women and young people. Fortunately, the party has since remedied that problem by placing the emphasis on antidiscrimination and affirmative-action provisions, where I believe it properly belongs.

More recently, the party prohibited the time-honored winner-take-all system of electing delegates whereby a candidate who had won a plurality of the popular vote in a state primary was entitled to all of its national delegates. It imposed instead a system of proportional representation under which each candidate who receives more than 15 percent of the vote is entitled to an equivalent share of the state's national delegates. This reform will undeniably achieve its goal of eliminating the inherent unfairness of winner-take-all at the state level, but the party left a huge loophole by permitting continued use of the winner-take-all practice at the congressional district level which may lead to even more disproportionate results than before. If proportional representation should achieve its stated purpose, however, it will inevitably make it more difficult for a candidate to win enough delegates to achieve a first-ballot nomination, thereby fostering what some think is the ironic possibility of creating the first convention to be "brokered" in the name of reform.

It is much easier to criticize the present nominating system than it is to come up with an alternative which corrects its many faults. Because of the constitutional nature of our political system and because every reform we attempt invariably brings with it unintended side effects, it is impossible to devise a perfect system. It may even be impossible to devise a good system. But it should be possible to come up with a system that is far superior to the one we have at present.

Before looking at alternatives, however, it is necessary to consider what we want to achieve in a nominating process. Here are some of the things I would like to see it contain:

☐ It should retain as its cornerstone the national nominating convention, which has served effectively as a vehicle for national intraparty conciliation and for giving the parties whatever degree of national identity they now have.

☐ It should offer the broadest possible range of candidates, and it should encourage or at least make possible the serious consideration of candidates who have neither the wealth nor the name recognition to be taken seriously at the outset.

☐ It should encourage the broadest and most direct possible participation by those persons who seek to affect their party's candidates and policies, but it should limit participation to those who choose to affiliate with that party.

☐ It should structure state primaries and conventions in a way that recognizes that candidates cannot contest for delegates in every state in the nation, and yet which will permit and perhaps even require each candidate to contest for delegates in a representative number of states in all parts of the country.

☐ It should provide a difficult but fair test of the candidates' judgment, appeal to different sections of the country, and even their stamina and ability to perform under pressure.

☐ It should above all be a *national* design, which permits no single state or region to cast an undue influence on the outcome and which focuses the candidates' and the country's attention on national concerns.

The acceptance of these criteria would obviously rule out adoption of a national primary system, which some people believe is the answer to the problem. A national primary would seriously if not completely undermine the value of the national conventions. It would also, I fear, give an inordinate advantage to those candidates who are already well known and who have greater access to campaign funds; it would virtually preclude consideration of lesser-known candidates. Too much would depend on a single roll of the dice, if you will, which presents a number of obvious dangers.

My own strong preference is for a series of regional primaries, probably six in all, separated from one another by either two or three weeks and held between mid-March and mid-June of election years. For example, a New England primary might start the process, to be followed several weeks later by one in the Middle Atlantic states, and followed successively by regional primaries in the South, the Midwest, the Rocky Mountain area, and the Far West. The order could be rotated every four years, so that no single region obtained a continuing advantage in the process. A state would not be required to hold a primary, but if it chose to do so, it would have to hold it on the day prescribed for its region. Interestingly, there is already some voluntary movement on the part of several states in the direction of regional primaries, particularly in the Pacific Northwest, which should give us some basis for evaluating the concept in 1976.

The adoption of a mandatory regional primary system would, I believe, bring a higher degree of rationality to a process which badly needs it. It would combine many of the strengths of the existing system with an orderly and more understandable structure. Such a system would no doubt have problems of its own, and no doubt some states with vested interests in the present system would vigorously resist its adoption, but I am convinced it would be a better system than that we now have, and better than any others that have been proposed.

Congress could enact such a system, of course, but so too could the national parties themselves, although this fact is not generally recognized. In January 1975, the U.S. Supreme Court decided in *Cousins* v. *Wigoda,* a case growing out of the refusal of the 1972 National Democratic Convention to seat Mayor Daley's Chicago delegates, that the national parties have the right to establish rules for the selection of delegates to their national conventions, even when those rules conflict with existing state laws. Although this case broke new legal ground, it is widely interpreted to give political parties authority in this area which they were never believed to have before. This authority, if the parties decided to use it, gives them a unique opportunity not only to fundamentally overhaul the nominating process in a rational way but also to give themselves new vitality and credibility. Obviously the two parties must work together to achieve a single system that would serve them both, but that need not be a major obstacle.

This task could be greatly assisted if President Ford, the first President in American history who has not been the product of the quadrennial nominating process and therefore the first to have no vested interest in its continuation, would take the initiative. I would like to see him appoint, in consultation with the leadership of both parties, a broadly based commission consisting of scholars, political figures and ordinary citizens to undertake an in-depth and comprehensive review of every aspect of our nominating procedures, to evaluate different alternatives, to explore the possibilities of widespread agreement on them, and to report back soon after the 1976 election. Without this kind of comprehensive national approach, I am convinced we will never achieve a rational and effective system. Nothing may come of such a commission, but I doubt it. Even if it proves impossible to agree on a new system, it is bound to produce a body of knowledge and experience that will tell us a great deal about what we have now and about how we might improve it. In any event, it is worth the effort, in my judgment, because the piecemeal, patchwork attempts at reform to date have not corrected the system's most serious shortcomings. I can think of no more worthy or appropriate undertaking in our nation's two hundredth year as we celebrate the blessings of our democratic system than to begin a serious effort to improve one of the most important elements of that system.

The postconvention period of a Presidential campaign presents an entirely different set of problems. Once he is nominated, the candidate need not worry about becoming known, about raising funds, about assembling a staff or building an organization. These goals are either already accomplished or well within reach.

The main problem comes from a different perspective altogether: keeping the candidates from succumbing to the temptation to transform themselves from flesh-and-blood human beings into the creations of a television studio. The challenge is in preventing, in effect, the short-circuiting of the democratic process by the electronic "selling of the President."

The Richard Nixon who was "sold" electronically during the 1968 campaign had gone through six primaries; he had attended numerous Republican Party functions; he had been touched by at least some of the people. Yet the temptation to avoid debate, to spurn real examination by the American people of his personality and programs was simply too great to resist. Indeed, he had given the American people a chance to examine him during 1960, and had probably lost the election as a result. And under current law regulating the communications media, there was absolutely nothing that could be done to enable the American people and the political opposition to draw out candidate Nixon and give the American people a fair chance to learn what his "secret plan" for Vietnam really was.

The media saw much of what was going on and attempted to communicate it. Efforts were made to draw Nixon into the open, to ask the tough questions, to let the American people know what he really stood for. The working press understands from firsthand experience the truth of Adlai Stevenson's lament that "the idea that you can merchandise candidates for high office like breakfast cereal . . . is the ultimate indignity to the democratic process." Because of this, the media have always been, and will continue to be, crucial in forcing candidates to open themselves to more scrutiny. They must continue this fight no matter how unwilling the candidate may be to comply.

Richard Nixon's unresponsiveness to the people continued with his 1972 Presidential campaign, which contrasted sharply with that of George McGovern. From the White

House came statement after statement on every conceivable issue, without the President ever condescending to appear to answer questions on them. The media tried their best to draw him out. They could not get to him, but they continued to cover his handouts and gave wide attention to his every pronouncement. The often brutal questioning to which the media constantly subjected George McGovern was certainly not matched by their treatment of Richard Nixon.

If a candidate is unwilling to face real questioning, should the print and electronic media be required to give attention to what he says? If there is no basis for learning with greater precision the background for the truth of what the candidate says, why should the media feel obliged to give his statements widespread attention?

Unfortunately, at least for the electronic media, present laws and regulations virtually dictate that a candidate who does not wish to have his views carefully examined still benefits from the exposure which inevitably is accorded the nominee of a major party.

Under the so-called fairness doctrine, the equal time provision, the political party rule and a variety of other statutory and Federal Communications Commission provisions, a candidate who wants to avoid real contact with the people or his opposition can do so with little difficulty. If he is an incumbent, the ability to reach the public without allowing the opposition similar broadcast exposure is even more striking.

The equal time provisions of the Communications Act of

1934 require broadcasters to give time to the candidates of
all parties for an office if the candidate of any party is given
such time. This effectively prohibits any possibility of televised debates between the major party candidates. Only in
1960 were those provisions waived by Congress. Worse still,
no matter how much an incumbent President may sound like
a candidate when he talks on issues, so long as he has not
formally announced his candidacy there is no obligation
created to spokesmen of the opposing political party. Even
when a President has been renominated by his party, his
ability to dominate the airwaves continues. As Newton
Minow, John Martin and Lee Mitchell note in *Presidential
Television*, the Republican National Committee in October
of 1964 attempted to obtain television time for Senator Barry
Goldwater after President Johnson delivered a major address
on foreign affairs. The networks refused, and the FCC
upheld their refusal, arguing that the subjects covered by
Johnson had been adequately covered in regular news
broadcasts. Yet as Minow and his co-authors indicate, "in
such major addresses delivered at the very height of the
campaign, a President has complete control over whether,
when, and for how long he appears on television; he reaches
a 'captive' audience on all three networks simultaneously;
and he is subject to no questioning or rebuttal. On the basis of
the decisions in the Eisenhower and Johnson cases, he can do
all this for free, without equal opportunities for his political
opponents."

If the dilemma of the opposition candidate is real, so is the problem of the oppostion party. Though the FCC has a "political party" doctrine, which in theory gives equal access to one party if another is either given or sold time to discuss issues or candidates, the commission has exempted Presidents from coverage under this doctrine. Therefore, if a President running for re-election uses television, the political party doctrine will not apply if the equal time law does not require an opportunity for the other party to reply. No matter what an incumbent President does, it is a "Catch-22" situation for the opposition party and its candidate.

Although there has been substantial improvement on the part of the television and radio networks in recent years in giving opposition viewpoints more visibility, these opportunities are still largely at the sufferance of the major networks. There is still no statutory basis on which a candidate or an opposition party can make their views known in a manner designed to give the American people better insights into the alternatives available.

Congress should take the lead in reclaiming television as a tool to be used by the people to *expand* their ability to judge the character, personality and policies of the people they elect to the Presidency. The leadership of the opposition party in Congress should be given the right to respond to any Presidential use of radio or television within forty-eight hours of that appearance, at an equally attractive time and on as many networks as were available to the President. And the right of the American people to see the candidates of the major political parties in open and free debate must be established by law. A simple repeal of the equal time provisions is not enough, for it still leaves in the hands of the television networks the frequency and format of any campaign debates.

Instead, legislation is needed to establish each major party's right to request up to five one-hour, simultaneous prime-time broadcasts on the three major television networks for purposes of debates among the candidates. Any other party that has polled something like 5 or 10 percent of the popular vote in the most recent Presidential election would also have the same right. This series of debates could begin shortly after the parties' nominating conventions and could extend throughout the ten-week campaign period from late August through early November.

Under this proposal, the Federal Election Commission established under the Federal Election Campaign Act of 1974 would receive requests from any candidate. This action would trigger automatic notification by the commission of other candidates who would qualify for such debates. In effect, the number of debates would be set by the highest number requested by any of the candidates of a qualifying party. This likely would result in the candidate of the party out of power requesting the maximum number of debates in any election year. Arrangements on debate details and format would be handled by the candidates, the networks and the Federal Election Commission. The commission would have final power to arbitrate any disputes on which agreement could not be reached by the candidates. Should any eligible candidate refuse to engage in one or more of the debates, the commission would be required to grant the use of that air time to those who have accepted, with no right of reply for any refusing candidate. The equal time provision would be suspended for the entire period covered by the proposal. And to defray the costs of these debates, Congress would appropriate funds to be paid the networks.

Under this proposal, a variety of debate formats could be used—ranging from head-to-head debates, to *Meet the Press*-type panel shows, to programs involving questioning by a wider range of citizens. But the common purpose would be to give the American public a better view of their candidates, and a clearer way of knowing when a candidate was trying to avoid scrutiny.

This proposal will not prevent candidates from pursuing their own expensive media campaigns. It will not force them to circulate among the American people during the campaign. Nor will it stop incumbents from using many of the advantages of their office. But we deserve a virtual guarantee that the American people will see the candidates confronting each other over a period of two months with regularity and, hopefully, in some depth. The media then would have the opportunity to question the candidates not only regarding the subjects they wish the people to hear about but also about those subjects which—while unpleasant or politically inopportune—may help balance the effects of massive publicity campaigns.

John Gardner wrote during the Nixon years that "President Nixon has created a curious and unprecedented one-way communication with the American people. He can reach us but we can't reach him. We can see him but he can't hear us. He is always with us but there is no dialogue." No single proposal can permanently reclaim the right of the American people to benefit from the airwaves. But attempts to open use of the media, to ventilate the issues, and to scrutinize the personalities and policies of potential Presidents can only increase public participation in the electoral process as well as Presidential accountability.

The election period can condition Presidents to believe that restraints on their power are few and insubstantial and that the rewards of isolation are many. Or it can become a time when Presidential candidates learn to accept the risks of openness and accountability and come to recognize these values as legitimate parts of our system.

The way we finance campaigns, the behavior of our parties, the effectiveness of the institutions used to choose our Presidents, and the role of the electronic media will continue to play a vital part in shaping the Presidential perspective. Each helps determine whether the candidate who achieves the Presidency will enter the office with a firm belief in the value of accountability to the electorate rather than to special interests, with an ability to view the parties and the media as legitimate institutions rather than unwelcome intrusions, and with a respect for the media as means for communication rather than as tools for political propaganda. And just as this period before election will affect the thinking of our Presidents, so it will determine whether the American people believe that their electoral process is worthy of a democracy and whether the person elected to the Presidency is responsive to the interests of that democracy.

3

The Presidential World-view

Presidents, Perquisites and Politics

But if you be affeared to hear the worst, then let the worst unheard fall on your head.
                              —*Shakespeare*, King John, *IV, ii*

The most important and least examined problem of the Presidency is that of maintaining contact with reality.
                              —*George Reedy*, The Twilight of the Presidency

Shortly after his inauguration, former President Eisenhower received a telephone call from General Omar Bradley, chairman of the Joint Chiefs of Staff. When the new occupant of the White House ended the call and put down the receiver, he remarked to his secretary, "He called me Mr. President, and I have known Brad all my life!" The walls of the White House already were beginning to close in.

If Omar Bradley's respect for the Presidency was typical, Dwight Eisenhower's bewildered response to that treatment probably was quite short-lived. From the moment a President takes his oath of office, the struggle for the Presidential soul begins. From the time he moves into the White House, his life is shaped by very basic factors that help determine his view of the world and the responses he must make to it.

Every President must learn to deal with the Congress, with his own political party and the opposition party as well, with the media and with many other institutions and individuals. But these relationships are colored and shaped by the way a President lives, his expectations about the need for facing the people for re-election and his ability to influence the choice of his successor. These basic ingredients of the Presidential view of the world are important, for they help determine the framework within which he views his other institutional relationships and the need for political responsiveness in those relationships.

Unfortunately, the modern-day Presidency has developed disturbing tendencies toward an isolated and extravagant life-style and toward a lessening of those basic political restraints which should constantly be present in the minds of our Chief Executives. None of these trends is decisive in shaping the Presidential office, but each contributes to a lessening of Presidential concern for and awareness of public opinion. If Presidents are remote and isolated in their life-styles, their perception of the public may be twisted. If

64

Presidents cannot run for re-election, their concern for public opinion may be lessened. And if Presidents can pick their own successors, their power in relation to the Congress certainly has been greatly enhanced.

The physical perquisites of the American Presidency have exploded in recent decades and have now enveloped our Presidency in a maze of staff, residences and property at his disposal.

No one would deny any President those physical perquisites of office necessary for the adequate performance of his duties. We would not deny him comfort. Presidents must be able to communicate instantly. They must have adequate security. They must be able to travel on important official business. But these legitimate needs do not justify the seemingly endless build-up of the physical resources surrounding the Presidency.

Over the past twenty-five years, Presidents have expanded their perquisites regardless of their ideologies or personalities or governing styles. In 1949, it was estimated that a personal income of about $3,500,000 would have been required to live President Truman's life-style. By 1973, the estimates on the real cost of running the Presidency had risen to between $70 and $100 million a year. Truman's fleet of planes numbered ten; by 1970, there were twenty-seven to fly the President and other top government officials around at an estimated cost of over $10 million per year. In that same period the cost of the domestic housekeeping staff at the White House had risen from about $150,000 to over $1,100,000 annually. The total appropriation for all White House staff in Truman's early years was under $700,000; by 1975, it was nearly $11 million. Indeed, the full list of the perquisites by the end of the Nixon Presidency was breathtaking: a full-time White House maintenance staff of seventy-five; more than twenty gardeners to care for the White House grounds; a 180-acre retreat, Camp David, which had been turned into a posh resort-like vacation home, complete with free-form swimming pool, bowling alleys, tennis courts, skeet ranges and a hundred and fifty sailors to guard it year-round; virtually unlimited entertainments funds, often paid for by a variety of other goverment agency budgets; a $35 million communications system linking him to any part of the world; a fleet of five 707 jetliners, sixteen helicopters and eleven Lockheed Jetstars; two $500,000 Lincoln limousines and over thirty other cars.

That Richard Nixon and his subordinates encouraged many excesses in the acquisition and use of these perquisites is less important than their ability to do so. They faced little initial opposition from the Congress and were virtually unaccountable in the spending of these funds. Their excesses are not likely to be repeated in the near future, but the residue of three decades will probably remain with us.

Compare the perquisites of our Presidents with the $50,000 per year salary that the Prime Minister of England draws, out of which he must pay all domestic bills, including the one housekeeper who resides at 10 Downing Street. The Prime Minister is of course not a head of state, but a head of government, while our Presidents exercise both functions. But surely we should consider whether we want our Presidents to live more like the Queen of England than the Prime Minister, into whose hands operational authority for running the government of that nation is vested. Unfortunately, the world's greatest democracy has allowed the trappings of monarchy to overgrow the office originally intended to be a protection against monarchical rule.

Presidents have not always lived like royalty. In the republic's early days, at least some of our Presidents lived like ordinary citizens. Thomas Jefferson woke in a small rooming house, dressed himself and walked to his own inauguration. After delivering his inauguration speech, he returned to his lodgings, only to find the luncheon table fully occupied. No one was asked—and no one volunteered—to give the President his place at the table. So Jefferson returned to his room, without his food but presumably with some sense of his mortality. President Polk, who saw many people during his day, once told a visitor that there were no kings in this nation, only "citizens who have been chosen by the people to manage the government for a limited time."

This notion led the late-nineteenth-century observer of American manners and mores James Bryce to marvel that:

> There is no servility, no fictitious self-abasement on the part of the citizens [in their relations to their Pres-

idents]. The spirit of equality which rules the country
has sunk too deep into every American nature for [any
President] to expect to be addressed with bated breath
and whispering reverence. He has no military guard, no
chamberlains or grooms-in-waiting; his everyday life is
simple. . . . He is surrounded by no such pomp and
enforces no such etiquette as that which belongs to the
governors even of second-class English colonies.

If only James Bryce could have met Richard Nixon.

Obviously, Presidents should not be required to live in
poverty. They must have resources adequate to perform
those duties given them by the Constitution. They should
have surroundings befitting a head of state. And as one still
haunted by the tragic events of President Kennedy's assassination over a decade ago, I recognize the need for adequate
Presidential security and its unfortunate by-product of
shielding our Presidents from everyday contact with the
American people.

But we must also recognize the dangers inherent in a
Presidential life-style that can lead those so inclined to
inhale the heady air of luxury and make it part of their
personality. The potential for damage is there, and much of
that potential was realized with the Nixon White House.
The endless obsession with luxury and comfort for the President must have played a part in isolating Richard Nixon
from the people. And the similar perquisites enjoyed by his
closest staff—the helicopters and limousines and airplanes

and all the rest—must have lessened their sensitivity in responding to the needs of the people.

Presidential personality can overcome the tendencies of the Presidential life-style, as we have seen with Gerald Ford. But to guard against a repetition of the Nixon years, we should attempt to inform the American people about the Presidential establishment and its possible dangers.

We could help the Congress and the people grasp the swollen nature of the modern-day Presidency by consolidating all the real costs of supporting it into one budget item. At present, the costs of the Presidency—the planes, the houses, the communications systems and, indeed, the White House staff—are scattered throughout the federal budget. No one *really* knows what it costs to support the Presidency. A consolidated Presidential budget would serve as a focal point around which to structure real public debate concerning the effect the Presidential establishment has on Presidential responsiveness and accountability. Consolidating the budget would also assist Congress in trimming waste where appropriate (such as limiting the number of Presidential residences) and would give the nation a continuing reminder that a huge Presidential establishment is one factor preventing us from restraining unaccountable Presidential conduct.

Perhaps more important than the view of the world that Presidents receive because of their physical surroundings is the influence of our system's most basic political restraints on the Presidential mind. Ironically, there is still a recurring notion that Presidents should be *more* insulated from politics—that if we want Presidents who are statesmen, we need to free them from the mundane worries of the political world. This, we are still told, would enable our Presidents to concentrate on the problems they face without sullying themselves in the political arena.

I believe that this view of the Presidency—while advanced with the best of intentions—is dangerous and misguided. It represents a lessening of the fundamental accountability that must be built into our political system. And it implicitly regards the people as a nuisance Presidents should be able to avoid, rather than as a constant source of wisdom and inspiration Presidents must actively seek.

One manifestation of this view of the Presidency is the proposal to limit our Presidents to a single, six-year term. The proposal has been advanced for many decades, never meeting with the favor of the American people. Five Gallup polls conducted on the six-year Presidency have shown a majority against its adoption in the Constitution. Perhaps significantly, the percentage of those in favor jumped from 19 percent in 1969 to 30 percent in July of 1973. Disillusionment with the Nixon re-election campaign of 1972 seems to have made the six-year concept more acceptable. If there had been no re-election campaign, people seem to have reasoned, there would have been no Watergate, no illegal campaign contributions and no dirty tricks. But if there had been no 1972 election campaign there probably also would have been no end to American troop involvement in the Vietnam War. And the absence of a 1968 campaign would likely have resulted in no reduction in the bombing of North Vietnam.

One of the few remaining ties Presidents have to politics is standing for re-election at the end of a four-year term. Remove that requirement, and one of the final restraints on unaccountable conduct is ended. It is not possible to isolate a President from political pressures and thereby make him better able to serve the public interest. Indeed, such pressures are the stuff of which the assertion of public interest is made. As Tom Cronin has observed, "The idea of a set single six-year Presidential term is the last gasp of those who cling to the hope that we can separate national leadership from the crucible of politics." Making Presidents into permanent lame ducks would loosen our Chief Executives from any restraints except those of personal whim or predilection.

Congress has begun to set restraints—through the Budget Control Act, the War Powers Act and other legislative measures—that should help to increase Presidential responsiveness. But we must recognize that elimination of the electoral test by the people would remove the force that most makes Presidents accountable.

As things are, the Twenty-second Amendment presents a serious enough problem because it removes necessary restraints from second-term Presidents. Both Richard Nixon and John Dean understood that late in 1972, just before Nixon's re-election to his last constitutionally permitted term. The former President told Dean that while he had not used the FBI or the Justice Department to harass political enemies thus far, "things are going to change now." While few other Presidents would use the impossibility of re-election as the pretext for invading Americans' civil liberties, the absence of that ultimate test cannot but help reduce any sense of Presidential prudence in the exercise of his powers.

If we are to restore a sense of Presidential perspective, repeal of the Twenty-second Amendment would make far greater sense than enactment of the single six-year term. It is simply wrong to eliminate re-election campaigns because of the abuses of one re-election committee. There is far greater merit in reforming our campaigns so that these abuses are less likely to recur, and in forcing our Presidents always to consider the implications of re-election.

When it comes to decreasing Presidential accountability, however, the Twenty-second Amendment pales beside the potential for damage presented by the Twenty-fifth Amendment. Twice in just more than a year, this amendment was invoked to fill vacancies in the Vice-Presidency. As we approach our bicentennial, we are in the extraordinary situation of having a President and a Vice-President in office on July 4, 1976, who were not elected by the people.

The problem of succession is a troublesome one, not amenable to easy solutions. Indeed, the history of the acts governing succession indicates the indecision that our nation has experienced over nearly two hundred years in attempting to fill vacancies in its two highest offices. The original Succession Act of 1792 gave the president pro tempore of the Senate the first opportunity to succeed to the Presidency, followed by the Speaker of the House and the Cabinet officers. In 1886, the President pro tem and the Speaker were eliminated from the line of succession, in favor of the Cabinet officers, with the Secretary of State first to succeed.

In 1945, it became clear that the provisions of the 1886 law were not good enough. When Harry Truman succeeded to the Presidency, a vacancy in the Vice-Presidency was created that was to last nearly four years. And the man who would have succeeded Truman had he died was the then Secretary of State, Edward R. Stettinius, Jr., a former chairman of the board of United States Steel, whose views were in no way similar to Truman's. While Truman could and did change Secretaries of State, the problems with the 1886 law had become apparent. In 1963, with the assassination of President John Kennedy, the revised succession law passed in 1947 at Truman's urging also showed its weaknesses. The Speaker of the House—who would have succeeded to the Presidency had Lyndon Johnson died—was John McCormack, then over seventy years old.

No one could have foreseen the bizarre events of 1973 and 1974 when the Twenty-fifth Amendment was being debated in the mid-1960s. The amendment clearly left open the possibility that both the Presidency and Vice-Presidency could be occupied by individuals not elected to those offices by the people. But now that this situation has come to pass, we must closely examine its implications.

The most unsettling aspect of the Twenty-fifth Amendment, of course, is that it allows a person who has not been freely selected by the American people to occupy either of the two highest offices in the land. But the amendment is also disturbing because it eliminates the grueling experience of the Presidential campaign. That experience is vital because it requires Presidential candidates to move throughout the country and acquaint themselves with a wide variety of people and ideas. And this process is most effective when an individual is running not as an incumbent President but as a candidate seeking that office. But the Twenty-fifth Amendment short-circuits the entire process.

Gerald Ford now can run in 1976 not as an aspirant for the Presidency who must suffer the tortures of a Presidential campaign as an ordinary citizen but rather as an incumbent able to manipulate people and institutions in a thousand different ways. If he so wishes, he can use the media to great advantage; he can avoid debate, and he can avoid discussion of the issues.

I frankly do not have the answers for solving the problems created by the Twenty-fifth Amendment. A variety of suggestions have been offered to deal with the three basic succession problems the amendment addresses: a vacancy in the

Vice-Presidency, a vacancy in the Presidency, and simultaneous vacancies in both offices.

In the case of a vacancy in the Vice-Presidency, the Twenty-fifth Amendment does not create great problems. I believe that the Congress adequately screened the nominations both of Gerald Ford and Nelson Rockefeller. As long as an appointed Vice-President does not succeed to the Presidency, no great harm has been done by virtue of the present provisions of the Twenty-fifth Amendment.

However, the accession of Gerald Ford to the Presidency raised the second of the three potential situations that must be evaluated—a vacancy in the Presidency. Whether a Vice-President succeeding to a vacated Presidency was appointed through the procedures of the Twenty-fifth Amendment, or whether he was elected with the President who died or resigned, I believe that changes are needed to assure greater accountability. Vice-Presidents selected through the Twenty-fifth Amendment have not had to face an electoral test of nationwide proportions. Even those selected through that electoral process are rarely examined carefully for their qualifications to fill the Presidency. The age of the Vice-President as regional or ideological ticket balancer is far from over. And while many of the individuals selected as Vice-President have been of the highest calibre, we should not trust to fortune what could be prevented through positive action.

Both in the situation of a Presidential vacancy and a dual

vacancy, the amendment presents major problems. Many differing suggestions have been offered, ranging from abolition of the Vice-Presidency to confirmation of all Vice-Presidents by the Congress to a special election to fill vacancies. All must be thoroughly explored. All present very substantial problems. But the troubling implications of the Twenty-fifth Amendment for the future of accountable Presidential government are so important that we must analyze all the possibilities and even consider devices not common to the American tradition, such as the special election. The motivation behind the Twenty-fifth Amendment was a good one; the results that it has brought could be disastrous. The need for change is pressing.

If our Presidents are to become less distant from political accountability to the American people, their perspective on the basic political realities they must face is important. So too are their day-to-day living styles and the perquisites of power which affect their view of the world. Both the perquisites of power and the politics of re-election and succession from the basic antennae with which Presidents feel the presence or absence of political and psychological restraints.

We should no more remove our Presidents from the basic check of re-election than we should allow them to appoint their successors. And we should do everything possible to make the Presidential life-style less isolating and less monarchical. Presidents with healthy personalities can successfully fight the tendencies of the office to increase the distance between them and the American public. But we should help insure that even those Presidents who might otherwise be tempted to use the Presidential life-style to barricade themselves from the people are less able to do so. And we should repeal the Twenty-second Amendment, change the Twenty-fifth Amendment, and reject the idea of a single Presidential term as fundamentally at odds with the concept of political accountability. Our Presidents' views of themselves and the political reality they face can and must become more compatible with responsible government and thereby help influence Presidential perceptions of the limits of proper behavior.

4

A Branch Divided

The President
and the Executive

*Everybody believes in democracy until he gets to the White House,
and then you begin to believe in dictatorship because it is so hard to
get things done. Every time you turn around, people just resist you
and even resist their own jobs.*
— *Kennedy White House aide, interviewed by Thomas Cronin*

By the early 1970s the administration of Richard Nixon had
largely transferred the powers and operating authority of the
Cabinet officers, designated by the Constitution as the chief
agents of Presidential power, to a large and unaccountable
White House staff. This development resulted in a further
and serious erosion of Presidential accountability to the
Congress and the American people.

The reasons for this shift are complex and date back many
decades. The movement of power from Cabinet officer to
White House staff was not a creation of Richard Nixon;

indeed, it had been developing for many years. Yet the Nixon administration distorted this trend to a point which threatened to totally remove Congress's ability to focus responsibility for policy development and implementation on officers who could be called to account for their actions. The Nixon White House staff, shielded by such defenses as "executive privilege" and "national security," and not required to be confirmed by the Congress or testify before it, formed a palace government almost completely removed from contact with the Congress and the people.

This increase in White House staff power posed serious dangers. Through law and tradition, Cabinet officers and heads of other executive branch agencies are far more open and accountable than the White House staff. Not only the Cabinet officers, but most other high-ranking officials within the departments are generally subject to Senate confirmation. Departmental programs must receive legislative authorization from the Congress and are subject to oversight by both Houses. Their budgets are similarly subject to examination by the Congress through the appropriations process. And by tradition, Cabinet and other executive branch officials are expected to respond to congressional committees when asked to testify and are generally available to the media for questioning. It is much more difficult for these departments and agencies to assert the awesome White House staff defenses of "executive privilege," "national security" and the "separation of powers." And the departments are staffed with career civil servants who are often available for private consultation with members of Congress and who are privy to essential information and often more amenable to disclose that information to the Congress and the media.

Almost none of this openness carries over to the White House staff. And during the Nixon Presidency, virtually every member of the Congress, at some point, experienced the frustration created by the lack of accountability in the White House. Policy decisions were centralized there, the Congress was almost totally excluded from any consultative processes, and Cabinet officers and their departments in most areas were often left without independent authority. The process became predictable. Two examples are illustrative of the Nixon White House style.

For over five years, I have been working for enactment of a Child Development Act to provide, on a voluntary basis, quality child care to the millions of American children whose parents are working or for children deeply affected by poverty. In 1971, those of us supporting this legislation conducted weeks of negotiations with then Health, Education and Welfare Secretary Elliot Richardson. The Secretary met with House and Senate conferees working on a final version of this legialation in late 1971. After a lengthy discussion, we agreed that the conferees would modify the bill under consideration and submit the modifications to him for comments. We did so, and he replied favorably regarding the revised version. Encouraged by this reply, the conference tentatively adopted the revised version and sent it to the Secretary for his official comments. When he suggested further modifications, we acceded to them and he indicated that he supported the revised bill and would do everything possible to get the President to sign it.

We felt that a compromise had been worked out in good faith which met the main objections of the administration while not violating the central purposes of the legislation. We thought we had an understanding, so on November 15 the conferees met for the final session, ratified this understanding, agreed to file the conference report, and adjourned the conference. But one week later, Senator Gaylord Nelson, chairman of the conference, received a letter from Secretary Richardson, dated November 18, in which the Secretary indicated quite clearly that he was no longer supporting this bill, regardless of our understanding.

Without ever mentioning the issues we had negotiated or the agreements we had reached, Secretary Richardson's letter suggested that he had misunderstood other provisions in the bill agreed to in conference and made it clear that the other provisions were unacceptable to him.

We may never know for sure why Secretary Richardson changed his mind, wrote that letter, and decided not to support the bill as he had previously agreed. But the general feeling in Congress was that Secretary Richardson did support the bill, went to the White House and urged that the bill be signed, and lost that argument to the people who ran the Domestic Counsel.

Predictably, on December 9, 1971, President Nixon vetoed the Child Development Act and now four years later, millions of children in this nation are still without the decent child care they so desperately need and deserve.

In one week, anonymous, unaccountable White House aides had reversed the work of Senate and House conferees dealing directly with the Cabinet Secretary whose responsibility it was to represent the administration position.

Similarly, in 1972, Secretary Richardson negotiated a compromise version of the Nixon administration's Family Assistance Plan with Senator Abraham Ribicoff of Connecticut. The compromise was agreed to and announced publicly, and the Secretary stated that he would go to the President and attempt to get him to help rally the Republican support necessary to get a bill adopted by the Senate. Shortly thereafter, the President stated that the compromise version reached by the Secretary with the Senate was unacceptable and that either the House version of this legislation was passed or a veto would follow. The practical and predictable result of this action was that no family assistance bill passed the Senate, thus no conference was possible and no bill could be enacted. Once again, the will of the Congress and the Cabinet had been thwarted by a White House staff accountable only to the President.

To me, these will always be examples of how Cabinet members, in the Nixon years, did not have the authority to negotiate with the Congress, and if they did negotiate and reach agreement, those agreements could be, and often were, reversed by the Domestic Counsel and the White House staff.

These were merely two instances of how policy was made during the Nixon years. The pattern was clear for all to see. As members of Congress, we worked on a particular piece of legislation with the appropriate Cabinet officer, believing that he should be the person representing the administration, since he was subject to Senate confirmation and general congressional oversight. Yet we found out that Robert Finch or Elliot Richardson or Claude Brinegar were often not in a position to make real commitments.

This, in turn, prevented the essential political and legislative process of give and take between the Congress and the administration from ever occurring in a meaningful way, and produced more vetoes and more misunderstanding than was necessary or desirable.

The transfer of Presidential authority from Cabinet to White House was probably even greater in the area of foreign affairs. It was clear that William Rogers, in his post as Secretary of State during much of the Nixon years, had no significant policy responsibility. Henry Kissinger, operating from the National Security Council within the White House, called the tune on virtually every significant foreign policy decision, whether dealing with the Middle East, Southeast Asia, India and Pakistan, or our relations with Western Europe and the communist superpowers. On those occasions when Secretary Rogers came to Capitol Hill to testify, his lack of authority became painfully obvious, and the Congress had virtually no way of probing Nixon administration foreign policy decisions. Henry Kissinger, of course, was unavailable for testimony.

This transfer of power and responsibility from the Cabinet and other executive departments to the White House represented a major decline in influence for these departments with the Congress. It meant that the Congress no longer was able to monitor executive branch actions by questioning the only truly accountable executive branch officials, the Cabinet officers and executive agency heads.

These executive branch officials must play an active role in formulating and administering Presidential policy. They should be influential policy advisors, listened to and respected by Presidents. But I do not believe that Cabinet officials can or should be independent agents, free to act without Presidential blessing. The President must have the ultimate power and authority to determine policy. And the most important role of the Cabinet or executive department head must be to possess the power and responsibility to represent the President's policies in dealing with his departments, the Congress, and the people. The Nixon White House, by removing this responsibility from the Cabinet, undermined Congress's prerogatives as well as the historic role of the executive branch officer.

The existence of the Cabinet as an institution, not established in the Constitution, rests primarily on custom, beginning in 1791 with the first group meeting of the President's principal executive officers. It is clear that Presidents, at least since the mid-nineteenth century, have never had much regard for the importance of the Cabinet as a collective institution. Abraham Lincoln, after drafting the Emancipation Proclamation, told his Cabinet, "I got you together to hear what I have written down. I do not wish your advise about the main matter, for that I have determined for myself." Woodrow Wilson, fifty years later, ignored his Cabinet on such crucial matters as the sinking of the *Lusitania* and even the declaration of war in 1917. And John Kennedy systematically disregarded the Cabinet as a policy body.

I do not believe that the Cabinet as an institution need have particular significance. But while the Cabinet was generally disregarded by Presidents, individual Cabinet officers were often consulted and were the agents of Presidential policy in dealing with their departments and with the Congress. They were presumably persons of high ability and stature, whose advice was important to the President. Part of the reason for their influence came from the simple fact that until quite recently Presidents had virtually no staff assistance of their own. Until 1929, Chief Executives were authorized the services of only one administrative secretary. That year, Congress provided two more secretaries and an administrative assistant. Herbert Hoover found this small staff an inconvenience, but for Franklin Roosevelt it was a disaster. In keeping with his Presidential style, Roosevelt's initial solution was an improvisation. Roosevelt simply gave men like Raymond Moley and Rexford Tugwell jobs in existing government agencies and cannibalized their time and talents to fit the needs of his expanding Presidency.

This *ad hoc* arrangement could not last forever, and so Roosevelt appointed a Committee on Administrative Management, headed by Louis Brownlow, to study the real need for a greater permanent White House policy staff. It concluded that "the President needs help"; its recommendations, however, clearly stressed the scope and responsibility of this assistance:

> These assistants, probably not exceeding six in number, would be in addition to his present secretaries, who deal with the public, with the Congress and with the press and radio. These aides would have *no* power to make decisions or issue instructions in their own right. They would *not* be interposed between the President and the heads of his departments. They would *not* be assistant Presidents in any sense . . . their effective-

ness in assisting the President will, we think, be directly proportional to their ability to discharge their functions with restraint. They would remain in the background, issue *no* orders, make *no* decisions, emit *no* public statements. [Emphasis added.]

The explosion in the number of the White House staff as agents of Presidential control over the growing bureaucracy began with these six assistants. Establishment of the Executive Office of the President in 1939, an outgrowth of the Brownlow commission's report to President Roosevelt, marked another milestone in the increasing power of the Presidency. Yet, clearly, in the minds of those who created that Executive Office, the need for Presidential staff was to foster accountability, not to enable Presidents to hide from it. The Brownlow report stated that the Executive Office "would materially aid the President in his work of supervising the Administrative agencies and would enable the Congress and the people to hold him to strict accountability for their conduct." The White House staff was to help increase the President's ability to respond to the other institutions of American government.

In thirty-five years, these admirable intentions became subverted by the growth of an instituion that now counts its employees in the thousands. From an initial appropriation of less than $1 million, the Executive Office has grown to a $100 million-per-year operation, with a staff of over 2,000 and an additional, unknown number of personnel "detailed" from other departments but actually working in the Executive Office.

Roosevelt's six staff assistants have grown to a cadre of several hundred, with sixty-five top-level positions paying $30,000 or more. This is the core of the President's policy staff, whose voices increasingly have drowned out those of the Cabinet officers and agency heads. This is the staff that in the Nixon administration saw the law as no obstacle to its goal of perpetuating the Nixon Presidency.

What had gone wrong in thirty-five years? What led most recent Presidents to feel the powerful need to allocate ever-greater responsibility to the White House staff at the expense of the Cabinet departments? One answer lies in the problem of the bureaucracy and its inertia and recalcitrance, which has gnawed at Presidents for many decades.

In 1816—the first year for which statistics exist—the executive branch had a total of 4,479 employees. By 1900 it had become a large force of over 200,000 and by the early 1970s a vast army of more than 2 million. The Presidency of George Washington, required to administer a grand total of nine federal programs, evolved relentlessly into the Presidency of Gerald Ford, with over 1,400 federal grant programs.

Presidents began to recognize early in the twentieth century that they were losing control of their own bureaucracy. President Taft lamented that while Presidents were the real head of government, "there seems to be an impersonal entity in the permanent governmental structure independent of him which in some degree modifies his responsibility for its operations. Chiefs of divisions and clerks of bureaus in the Civil Service in Washington have been there for decades. They are loyal to the government and not especially beholden to any one President."

And Taft's lament of 1910 became Harry Truman's lament of 1950: "I thought I was the President, but when it comes to these bureaucracies, I can't make them do a damn thing," and, "Every President in our history has been faced with this problem: how to prevent career men from circumventing Presidential policy."

Perhaps Henry Kissinger put this view most starkly: "First of all, you have to weaken the bureaucracy. They all want to do what I am doing, so the problem becomes, how do you get them to push papers around, spin their wheels, so that you can get your work done." The bureaucracy—and the typical Cabinet member heading that bureaucracy—has become an obstacle to be maneuvered around rather than a source to be consulted.

Presidential concern over bureaucratic unresponsiveness is often well founded. The inertia caused by the layering of executive branch decision-making can be unbelievably frustrating. And the attitude of independence from Presidential authority often found in the bureaucracy poses a serious and unquestioned threat to establishing accountability for Presidential policy. In the debates over the Constitution, the framers discussed the relative wisdom of a single President or a multiple form of leadership and decided to concentrate authority and responsibility in one person. Yet the attitude of independent authority so common to the bureaucracy undermines this unitary leadership concept by reducing the Congress's ability to focus this responsibility on our President.

In addition, the executive branch and its departments are organized with authority dispersed widely and irrationally, so that the President is often unable to find in one Cabinet officer someone with full authority to implement a particular key policy.

All too often, present-day problems force Presidents to rely too heavily on non-Cabinet department resources simply because the present structure of the Cabinet and other executive departments is not capable of dealing with new problems. The energy dilemma is one example of interdepartmental confusion and lack of coordination. Energy policy-making responsibility is spread among the departments of the Interior, Treasury, Transportation, Commerce, State, Defense and the Federal Energy Administration. To learn about an international economic matter relating to energy, the Treasury and State departments must be consulted. To find out about transportation policy as it relates to energy usage, the Transportation Department is the key. The Defense Department has jurisdiction over our nation's

naval petroleum reserves. And so it goes, leading to a bureaucratic maze that often paralyzes action and leads to
White House frustration.

Some recent Presidents have attempted to solve this
problem by requesting the Congress to authorize a more
rational organization of the executive branch, requests
which Congress has generally ignored. Others have simply
not attempted to solve the problem. But the result in both
cases has been the development of a new executive branch
within the White House, beyond the reach of the Congress,
vested in high-paid political appointees responsible only to
the President. This staff has been given the power to go far
beyond the original restrictions of the Brownlow Commission and involve itself in matters properly the responsibility
of executive department officers.

Congress must bear a heavy burden of responsibility for
this development. We have often been unresponsive to
Presidential pleas for legislative authority to reorganize the
executive branch along more modern lines. And we have
allowed the Executive Office of the President to grow enormously, while only rarely subjecting its budget to any scrutiny by congressional appropriating committees. Some of the
most important jobs in the Executive Office of the President
are still not formally authorized by the Congress. By con-
trast, most programs and departments have a formal legislative authorization which creates them and then receive
money for operations through the appropriations process.

This legislative authorization is important because it involves two additional congressional committees, with their specialists in the particular program area, allows legislative oversight by those committees, and requires justification of the activity when the authorization is up for renewal.

Yet only in 1974 did Congress even seriously consider legislation requiring legislative authorization for top-level White House offices. For too long, the Congress let itself be lulled into compliance with White House wishes on staffing for the President. Comity between the branches of government, we were told, required that we not look at the authority for the White House staff positions or the budgets for those positions. Yet for too long, "comity" meant that the White House has been given whatever it wanted. And unless Congress uses its power to authorize programs and appropriate money, comity becomes "comedy"—a cruel joke slowly sapping the vitality out of any possible system of restraints on unaccountable Presidential power. There is no better recent example of Congress's failure to exercise its responsibilities, coupled with an administration determined to subvert the role of competing governmental institutions within our society, than the development of the Office of Management and Budget and the Domestic Council within the Nixon administration.

In 1970, President Nixon forwarded Reorganization Plan #2 to the Congress. This plan, which established the Office of Management and Budget and the Domestic Council, was adopted over some dissent in the House, but with virtually no discussion in the Senate. In the years that followed, the consequences of this reorganization became all too clear.

The Bureau of the Budget traditionally had been an important staff arm of the President. It helped him in the coordination, formulation and administration of the federal budget, as well as in the resolution of certain types of interagency problems. As the National Academy of Public Administration recently noted, "The bureau functioned as a catalyst and coordinator. It was perceived generally as a center of expertise and source of trusted advice. Its staff was regarded as an elite, nonpartisan professional corps of dedicated public servants. . . ."

Even before the bureau was reorganized in 1970, the growth of the White House office staff under the Nixon administration had robbed it of a good deal of its program advisory responsibility. This raid was completed with President Nixon's Reorganization Plan #2. Immediately, political officials loyal to the White House began to penetrate the OMB staff in important positions. The career staff was shunted aside, and OMB became a powerful policy-making force outside the reach of the Congress or the people.

What OMB did not carve out for itself, the Domestic Council did. Ostensibly created to facilitate the coordination of interdepartmental disputes and to improve the efficiency of governmental programs, the Domestic Council under John Ehrlichman soon acquired a staff of over seventy. Its executive director was not subject to confirmation. Although part of the White House Office, it stripped Cabinet officers and departments of their policy-making authority and even became involved—through Egil Krogh and Gordon Liddy —in illegal covert activities. The Domestic Council committees, which in theory were designed to allow various Cabinet members to work together on problem-solving, became meaningless as the power of the council staff grew.

This shift totally perverted the "strict accountability" goal of those who created the Executive Office of the President. As the National Academy for Public Administration concluded, "The principal assistants and counselors [to the President] have been converted from intimate personal advisors to the President to the equivalent of assistant Presidents, managing the executive establishment out of the White House."

Of course, this shift from accountability to arrogance had not been accomplished overnight. But even when it became apparent that the White House staff, and the Domestic Council in particular, had acquired too much power, Congress refused to reassert its most basic weapon: the power of the purse. In September 1973, I attempted to cut the appropriation for the Domestic Council from $1.1 million to $350,000. I recognized the valid need for coordination among departments, a purpose for which the Domestic Council had been established in 1970. Yet it was now clear that the Domestic Council had become the shadow government under John Ehrlichman. On the day my amendment was considered by the Senate, I held up a copy of the *Washington Star,* which ran a banner headline reporting the indictment of Mr. Ehrlichman and two former Domestic Council staff employees, Egil Krogh and Gordon Liddy, on charges relating to the burglary of Dr. Daniel Ellsberg's psychiatrist's office.

But the issue went beyond whether two members of the Domestic Council staff had been involved in illegal activity. At stake was whether Congress would merely wait for a President who felt no need for an Ehrlichman-like Domestic Council, or whether we would assert our own power of the purse, thus sending a clear signal to the White House that power in the executive branch must be returned from the White House staff to the Cabinet departments and executive agencies. As I said in Senate debate on my amendment, "The Nixon Domestic Council was designed to place in the White House a staff which the President picked on his own, with no confirmation requirement of the Senate, with a budget and money for which they were not held accountable, which could hide behind principles of separation of power and executive privilege as defined by the President, to do, to put it mildly, any damn thing they wanted to do." Despite the clear dangers and abuses of the Domestic Council, my amendment was defeated by nearly two to one. Another amendment that I offered on that same day sought to eliminate $1.5 million White House "special projects" funds. It was also defeated, even though the Nixon White House refused to reveal to the Congress how this money had been spent, and even though there was strong evidence that some of the money in that fund was used to finance the illegal "plumbers" operations.

The arguments raised against both amendments were the same, tired protestations of the need for "comity" between the executive and legislative branches that had prevented thorough congressional scrutiny of White House office budgets for decades. As one opponent of my amendment put it, "Let us bear in mind that to cut the President's request and all the instruments that he needs in order to effectively carry on his duties . . . is similar to the President's trying to dilute or cut appropriations made by our committees here in Congress. The element of comity between the executive and the legislative branches of government enters into this picture." What he failed to mention, however, is that the constitutional authority to spend rests exclusively with the Congress. We have the power to spend; it is Congress's most effective weapon against executive abuse.

Presidential frustration and congressional timidity had combined to enable the Nixon White House staff to totally dominate the executive branch. This transfer of authority from Cabinet to White House had serious implications for the ability of Congress and the American people to be more fully informed of executive branch actions and to focus responsibility for those actions on officers accountable to the Congress.

Gerald Ford's White House has made some laudable efforts to reverse the flow of authority out of the Cabinet departments which had taken place in the Nixon years. But any such effort will be of only limited, and probably temporary, value unless we can make changes that will transform Cabinet and other executive branch officers into more powerful and responsible agents of Presidential policy, and make the departments into more modern and useful tools for policy development and implementation.

This does not mean that our Presidents have no need for a White House staff. They clearly do. But the creation of competing institutions in the White House with the authority to bypass the executive departments inevitably leads to a lessening of executive branch responsibility to the Congress and to the American people.

If these executive branch officers are bypassed, one of the most valuable dialogues in American political life will be eliminated. The learning process that takes place between executive branch officer and congressman is a two-way process. We live in a representative system of government, and the Congress is elected by the people as their representatives at the federal level. If the executive is to learn from the Congress about the differing wants and needs of the American people, we need a constant dialogue between executive and Congress. And through this dialogue the Congress too can become more aware of the difficulties and realities facing administrators of federal programs on a day-to-day basis. But if authority is transferred from the executive departments to the White House staff, this dialogue becomes sterile and meaningless. The losers are the American people.

A number of fundamental steps are needed if the return of authority from the White House staff back to Cabinet departments is to become a permanent feature of the executive branch.

The persistent and very real frustration of Presidents of both parties with a bureaucracy they often regard as sluggish and outdated must be remedied. The bureaucracy has a right to present its point of view, which should be given full consideration by a President in making key decisions. But that right does not extend to outright obstruction, which so often occurs. Richard Nixon felt a tremendous frustration upon entering office that the vast federal bureaucracy was predominantly made up of Democrats named during the great expansion of federal programs throughout the Kennedy and Johnson years. That frustration was legitimate, for any President has the right to attempt to carry out the mandate he feels the country has given him and move federal programs in his desired direction, consistent with the law. He has the responsibility and the right to try to deliver on that mandate, *so long as* he does so legally and the Cabinet and other department heads remain in operational control of the development and implementation of Presidential policies within their departments.

That President Nixon often disregarded the law and undermined the authority and control of executive departments does not lessen the basic validity of his frustration, which was fervently shared by previous Presidents. I remember talking to an assistant to John Kennedy during the early years of his administration, when I was attorney general of Minnesota. I asked him about the possibility of getting the Defense Department to implement a policy that would favor small businesses in economically depressed areas. His response was that he didn't even know how to get a pencil out of the Defense Department, much less a policy.

Ending this frustration will require that the bureaucracy become more, not less, politically responsive to Presidents. We need more policy-responsive political appointees, running deeper into the bureaucracy and working alongside civil servants. But the primary responsibility and accountability of these political officers should be to the Cabinet Secretary. And Congress should be far more receptive to Presidential pleas for executive branch reorganization and more sympathetic to the constant Presidential frustration with the organization of congressional committees.

Unless the Cabinet is restructured to reflect today's needs more adequately, the Cabinet departments can never reach their greatest efficiency. While the precise nature of Cabinet

99

revisions requires much study, that study should be begun and action taken. And it should be a joint venture of the Congress and the executive, coupling study of a Cabinet restructuring with study of a similar congressional committee restructuring. The Congress has many of the same problems now present in the executive branch—a lack of clear committee jurisdictional lines and an overlapping of many committee responsibilities. If we worked together to develop an executive-legislative reorganization plan, which meshed Cabinet departments with congressional committee jurisdictions, we might well make both more responsive to the American people.

The more complete the sphere of authority of the Cabinet officers in dealing with major policy problems, the more likely future Presidents will be to deal with them rather than a staff member in the White House. And the more relevant and helpful these Cabinet department officers are to future Presidents, the better the executive branch will be able to relate to the Congress.

To make these executive branch officers more responsive to the Congress, we should expand the scope of their appearances before us. Institution of a question-and-report period in the Senate, along the lines of parliamentary practice, would help.

By subjecting Cabinet officers to questioning before the entire Senate—and making this available to radio and television—a question-and-report period might force Presidents to nominate stronger Cabinet officers and give the entire Senate the opportunity to question them closely.

In exchange for a congressional effort to make the executive and legislative branches more responsive to modern needs, the Congress should insist on a clear definition of the authority and size of the White House staff. For too long, these jobs have been simply funded yearly, with little oversight as to how the money was being used. Finally, in 1974, the Senate and House passed strong legislation giving us for the first time legislative authority over top White House jobs. It required the White House to tell Congress what those individuals were doing, and it set a June 30, 1978, cutoff date on the authorization for these staff positions. This latter provision was particularly important, since it would require our next President to justify his need for White House staff assistance periodically, as the authority legislation required extension. This legislation did not become law, although both Houses passed it, because conferees could not agree on an extraneous amendment. Because it is vitally needed, I am confident it will become law in the 94th Congress. It would not solve our problems in this area, but it would begin to give Congress greater oversight of the budget and staff within the White House.

In addition to finding out more about what is going on within the White House, we should also declare certain types of White House activities off limits. Presidents need a small, lean staff to help develop Presidential policies. But when that staff becomes so large and so structured that it removes functional authority and responsibility from Cabinet officers, the limits of proper White House activity have been crossed.

The line here is not always a clear one, but it could be clarified somewhat by abolishing bodies such as the Domestic Council and the Council on International Economic Policy. If the Cabinet departments were properly reorganized along modern lines, much of the coordinating role which these White House offices supposedly perform could be eliminated and greater authority restored to the Cabinet departments. At the very least, if bodies such as the Domestic Council cannot be eliminated, Senate confirmation of their directors should be required. And prohibiting any individual from holding both a Cabinet positon and a top White House position—as Henry Kissinger has done for years, as Secretary of State and head of the National Security Council—would prevent use of the White House shield to avoid facing full congressional responsibility.

If these actions were taken, both the President and the Congress would benefit. The President would be able to name more political appointees in the bureaucracy to help carry out Presidential politics, and he would get a reorganized and, hopefully, more effective executive branch and congressional committee structure. The Congress would receive in exchange closer questioning of Cabinet officers, through the question-and-report period, and clear limits on the White House staff. These limitations should attempt to reestablish the White House staff's role as the Brownlow commission report in 1937 saw it: to aid Presidents but not to become duplications of Cabinet officers within the White House. Thereby, the executive departments will be strengthened and Congress and the people better able to hold the President accountable for his actions.

We must be realistic in our expectations of how much changes in White House–executive branch relations can achieve. Presidents will continue to need a tough White House staff to help develop policy options and give them the political advice they need.

Changes in the structure of the Cabinet departments and the authority of the Cabinet and other executive branch officers can help the Congress, however, to enforce more accountability from our Presidents. By making the executive departments more politically responsive and more useful organizationally to the President, these changes can reduce the Presidential impulse to concentrate power in the White House staff. And by defining the legal limits of power and authority for White House staffs, and restricting them to a more circumscribed role, the Congress will be better able to carry on its vital dialogue with Cabinet and executive branch officers.

We can force Presidents to speak and act through agents who must come before the Congress and justify their administration's action; who cannot hide behind the shield of "executive privilege" or "national security"; who cannot avoid the tough questions that must be answered. And the more opportunity the Congress has to exercise oversight over executive branch actions through these executive branch representatives, the less likelihood there will be of another Watergate taking shape behind the high walls of the White House.

5

The President
and Congress

The Decline of
Congressional Power

An elective despotism was not the government we fought for, but one which should not only be founded on free principles but in which the powers of government should be so divided and balanced amongst several bodies of magesties as that no one could transcend their legal limits without being effectually checked and restrained by the others.

—Thomas Jefferson

[Congress] has come to be a sometimes querulous but essentially kindly uncle who complains while furiously puffing on his pipe but who finally, as everyone expects, gives in and hands over the allowance, grants the permission, or raises his hand in blessing, and then returns to his rocking chair for another year of somnolence broken only by an occasional anxious glance down the avenue and a muttered doubt as to whether he had done the right thing.

—Former Representative Carl Vinson, 1962

By the late 1960s, thoughtful observers of the American political scene began to wonder whether Congress was capable of being coequal with the other branches of government. Its influence was rapidly declining in the face of an

105

ever more powerful and assertive executive branch. The sticky questions could no longer be avoided. Was the decline of congressional power and influence only a temporary phenomenon or had something fundamental taken place under the pressures of growing domestic and geopolitical problems that forever would lessen Congress's ability to restrain Presidential conduct? If only temporary, how could Congress's proper role as a part of a meaningful system of restraints be restored? And if the causes were more basic and permanent, what substantial chance remained to continue the American experiment in representative government?

The cause for concern was—and still is—a real one. Over a period of decades, the power of the Congress—intended to be both a force for positive government and the principal check against executive branch tyranny—had been systematically eroded and weakened. A potent combination of Presidential action and congressional inaction had shifted the balance of power, particularly in foreign affairs, undercutting much of Congress's role as a restraint against the arbitrary exercise of Presidential power.

Congress's forceful exercise of its basic powers was endangered by its inability to wield the restraining powers designed to prevent the President from dominating the American governmental process. Each of these constitutionally conferred congressional powers often seemed to be ineffective; each was vitally important if a sense of balance was to be restored to governmental actions; and each seemed increasingly to come under the control of an unrestrainable executive branch.

The Constitution granted Congress extensive powers. Among others, it gave Congress the power of the purse, the power to declare war, to control interstate and foreign commerce, to ratify treaties, to override Presidential vetoes, to investigate, to indict and remove public officers through impeachment, to confirm Presidential nominees for key offices, and to make all laws "necessary and proper" for carrying into effect these other powers. These powers were there, waiting to be exercised. The questions that confronted the nation as the Presidency of Richard Nixon began to unfold were whether Congress had the will to exercise them and whether the executive could change the fundamental balance of these powers.

To the Founding Fathers, no power granted to Congress was more potent than the power of the purse. As James Madison said, "This power over the purse may in fact be regarded as the most effectual weapon with which any Constitution can arm the immediate representatives of the people for obtaining a redress of every grievance and for carrying into effect every salutary measure."

Under the Nixon administration, the executive branch moved to nullify this power over the purse through new departures in the old practice of impounding funds. The impoundment practice dates back in one form or another to the administration of Thomas Jefferson. But Presidents generally had used it for recognizable and often valid purposes, such as responding to specific congressional directives or exercising fiscal or programmatic prudence in the expenditure of military or weapons funding.

Although Presidents since Ulysses S. Grant had sought authority to use the item veto as a means of establishing their spending priorities, that power never had been granted. Indeed, the Constitution specifically gave the President power to veto only entire appropriations bills—not items within such legislation which a President deemed offensive. This distinction is not merely a technical one but has profound significance in determining the relative powers of Congress and the President. A line-item veto of appropriations bills leaves Congress with vastly less authority over expenditures, because it allows Presidents to pick and choose particular items they deem offensive, items almost always included in much broader appropriations bills. As one example, the Legal Services program, for which I have fought for years, is vital in helping millions of poor Americans obtain equal justice under law. The program has powerful opponents who object to attempts to use government funds to correct legal wrongs. To help insulate the program from political pressures, the Congress in 1974 established a Legal Services Corporation to operate the nationwide legal assistance program. Allowing a President the power to line-item veto the appropriation for the Legal Services Corporation, which amounts to only $96 million out of a State-Justice-Commerce appropriations bill of over $6 billion, would vastly increase the difficulty of Congressional supporters to override that veto. If a President must veto the entire appropriations bill, on the other hand, support for the Legal Services program can coalesce with support for other equally important programs and increase the possibility of Congress's prevailing.

Richard Nixon apparently decided that although the Constitution did not confer on him the line-item veto power, he would arrogate that power to himself through the use of impoundments, by which he would largely strip Congress of its power of the purse. This marked a definite and important break with past Presidential practice. As Louis Fisher observed in 1972, funds generally had been "withheld either in response to specific statutory directives or on grounds of prudent use of funds in weapons procurement. An entirely different situation has developed under the Nixon Administration, where funds have been withheld from domestic programs because the President considers those programs incompatible with his own set of budget priorities."

The stream of Nixon impoundments was steady. By the end of his first term, more than a hundred federal programs were affected by them. At one point, they reached over 20 percent of the controllable sector of the domestic federal budget. Programs for which impoundment or its functional equivalent was used included food stamps, rural water and waste disposal grants, Rural Electrification Administration loans, $6 billion in sewage treatment funds voted by the Congress over a Nixon veto, highway construction monies, Farmers' Home Administration disaster loan funds, HUD contract authority, manpower training programs, Indian Health Service funds, Indian education funds, library resource money, veterans' cost-of-education grants and a variety of other programs.

One of the most outrageous examples of this technique occurred in my state of Minnesota. I fought successfully to have farmers who had suffered from natural disasters included in disaster legislation considered by the Congress in 1972 as a result of the damage brought about by Hurricane Agnes. When this provision was signed into law, farmers in my state who had lost their crops because of flooding had every reason to believe that they would be helped.

Following floods and very serious wet field conditions in the spring of 1972, Secretary of Agriculture Earl Butz designated fourteen Minnesota counties eligible for Farmers' Home Administration (FHA) emergency loans on June 26, 1972. Farmers were told that loan applications would be received and processed until June 30, 1973, and they were encouraged to delay filing until after the final harvest to be sure all losses were included. Relying on this, many Minnesota farmers delayed filing.

Contrary to the law, on December 27, 1972, the Agriculture Department suddenly announced that these funds were being eliminated. On that same date, Secretary Butz directed the state FHA office not to accept any more applications from the counties previously designated eligible. Thousands of Minnesota farmers who had relied on previous administration assurances were suddenly denied eligibility for assistance despite the law.

Fortunately, court action succeeded in restoring much of the program, just as more than twenty other court decisions went against Nixon administration impoundments. But the willingness of that administration to use impoundment in violation of the law indicated that this tool had taken a new and ominous turn.

If new types of impoundments threatened the congressional power of the purse by the early 1970s, years of Presidential war-making with only limited congressional consultation similarly threatened Congress's important war-making powers.

The framers of the Constitution, though they disagreed on many things, seemed quite united on the importance of keeping this power within the Congress. For Hamilton, the President's authority as Commander-in-Chief would be "much inferior" to that of the British king, and would amount to nothing more than "the Supreme command and direction of the military and naval forces as first general and admiral." The powers of declaring war and raising and regulating armies "would appertain to the legislature." For

Madison, there could be no opposition to the "simple, the received, and the fundamental doctrine of the Constitution, that the power to declare war, including the power of judging the causes of war, is fully and exclusively vested in the legislature, that the Executive has no right in any case to decide the question whether there is or is not cause for declaring war." Even for Jefferson, the "dog of war" had been given an effectual check "by transferring the power of letting him loose from the executive to the legislative body."

Despite the clear language of the Constitution and this impressive body of opinion, modern Presidents have been exceedingly inventive in their ability to circumvent the congressional war-making power. In 1964, Congress had passed a permission slip for Presidential war-making in Vietnam on the basis of probably misleading information; a secret air war in Cambodia had been waged in 1969 and 1970 resulting in over 100,000 tons of bombs being dropped with no formal congressional authorization or knowledge; the U.S. military operated in Laos without formally notifying the Congress, and when asked under what authority those military personnel were operating in Laos, the State Department replied that "they are there under the executive authority of the President."

Congress must bear a heavy responsibility for the deterioration of its own war-making power. We knew what was going on in Vietnam, even though those voting on the initial Gulf of Tonkin resolution may not have voted with full awareness of the circumstances surrounding the incident that led to its passage. During each appropriation struggle over Vietnam funds, we were aware of the implications of our vote. But the overwhelming and very understandable impulse not to leave American troops without adequate support overcame the views of all but a few of those members of Congress who were opposed to the war.

Unfortunately, outright deception also played a part in undermining the congressional war-making powers. There is a strong suspicion that the events surrounding the Gulf of Tonkin resolution may have been misrepresented to the Congress. The secret air war in Cambodia and the revelations of a secret "tilt" toward Pakistan during the Indian-Pakistani war in 1971 also indicated a disposition on the part of the President to use both muscle and deception in an attempt to work his will on the Congress.

Similarly, Presidents have largely subverted the significance of the treaty ratification powers of the Constitution through use of the so-called executive agreement, often entered into secretly and not requiring ratification by the Senate. This dramatically shifted the power to make agreements with foreign nations from Congress to the executive. Treaty ratification contemplates agreements with foreign governments mutually consented to by President and Congress; executive agreements are entered into by Presidents without any congressional assent.

The growing use of executive agreements clearly shows

their popularity with recent Presidents. In 1930, the United States concluded 25 treaties and 9 executive agreements. But in 1971, the Nixon administration concluded 214 executive agreements and only 17 treaties. And of perhaps greater importance than the dramatic numerical shift to use of executive agreements, which did not require ratification by the Senate, was the shift to this type of document for the important diplomatic business of the United States. While the Senate was sent treaties and asked to ratify often trivial international agreements, the White House disposed of base and mutual-aid agreements affecting the future of American foreign policy with no effective congressional input.

During the 1960s and early 1970s, the Senate disposed by treaty of such "crucial" issues as the preservation of archeological artifacts in Mexico, a protocol relating to an amendment to the International Civil Aviation agreement, the Locarno agreement establishing an international classification for industrial designs, a treaty relating to international classification of goods and services to which trademarks are applied, revisions of international radio regulations, and an international agreement regarding maintenance of certain lights in the Red Sea.

Yet Congress was not informed about the secret agreements or understandings pledging American assistance that President Nixon apparently entered into with former South Vietnamese President Thieu in 1973, at the time of the signing of the Paris Peace Accords. And the Senate subcommittee involved with such matters had no knowledge of vital executive agreements in 1960 with Ethiopia, in 1963 with Laos, in 1964 with Thailand, in 1966 with Korea, and in 1967 with Thailand.

Congress was not without substantial blame for this development. In 1953, Secretary of State John Foster Dulles, after consulting with congressional leaders, told President Eisenhower that he could proceed to organize a system of military bases "without further authority, particularly as future commitments for funds are subject to congressional appropriations." Congress permitted its treaty-making power to atrophy, relying instead on a power of appropriations that also has rarely been exercised. Congressional timidity thus nurtured the further expansion of unrestrained Presidential power.

If the Congress was less than assertive in claiming its constitutional ratification prerogatives in the making of treaties, it often seemed equally unconcerned with its power to confirm Presidential nominations for key government posts.

Hamilton saw in this power a check on the Presidential urge to nominate those "who had no other merit than that of coming from the same state to which he particularly belonged or being in some way or other personally allied to him or of possessing the necessary insignificance and pliancy to render him the obsequious instruments of his pleasure." Nevertheless, by the early 1970s, the Nixon administration had nominated and the Congress had confirmed a generally undistinguished Cabinet. And we had created many powerful White House offices—such as the Domestic Council, the Council on International Economic Policy, and the Office of Management and Budget—whose heads were not required to undergo the processes of senatorial confirmation.

Occasionally, the Congress did show the power of the confirmation device. In rejecting the Supreme Court nominations of Clement Haynesworth and G. Harrold Carswell, the Senate showed a willingness to assert congressional rights in the making of key nominations. I believe that congressional pressure at his confirmation hearings made former Interior Secretary Walter Hickel more sensitive to environmental problems than he otherwise might have been. And the withdrawal of L. Patrick Gray III's nomination as FBI Director, after testimony at his Senate confirmation hearings revealed his likely involvement in the Watergate investigation cover-up, also showed the potential power of the confirmation process. Indeed, the very absence of any requirement for confirmation of heads of such White House offices as the Domestic Council and the Office of Management and Budget was a major factor in the increasing isolation of real policy-making power in the Nixon White House staff.

The confirmation power is only one part of what is undoubtedly one of our most important congressional powers —the ability to investigate and conduct thoroughgoing oversight of the executive branch. When the Congress exercised this power, the results were often impressive. The Senate Watergate Committee hearings, the hearings conducted in 1966 and 1968 on Vietnam by the Senate Foreign Relations Committee, and the House Judiciary Committee's impeachment proceedings all demonstrated the power and effectiveness of searching investigation of the executive branch.

Yet, too often, the Congress has failed to exercise the power of investigation early enough. Had we been more diligent in pursuing some of the apparent excesses of the Nixon White House in 1969 and 1970, perhaps the Judiciary Committee's impeachment investigation might never have been necessary. Had we more searchingly probed the initial entanglement of the United States in Vietnam in the early 1960s, perhaps the need for the 1968 hearings—when over 500,000 American troops were committed—might have been obviated.

The decline of the congressional investigatory and oversight power also had disastrous effects on the accountability of American government. Presidential assertion of the so-called doctrine of executive privilege, so vital to the maintenance of unaccountable Presidential power, ballooned in the Nixon administration. His administration invoked the "doctrine" twenty-nine times through early 1973, compared to two times in the Kennedy administration and three times in the Johnson years.

The fault here was not Congress's alone. But the Nixon administration's use of executive privilege probably could not have succeeded as well as it did had there been a more vigorous congressional challenge to each new assertion of executive branch powers.

Congress's responsibility to oversee operation of the many domestic programs launched in the mid-1960s had not been used to the fullest because of a failure to employ sophisticated performance accounting techniques to ensure efficiency. As a result, the Congress's standing with the public was diminished by a President who claimed that only he could ensure significant savings and increased efficiency in meeting domestic programmatic objectives.

And the failure of the Congress to oversee the mushrooming of the Executive Office of the President and the explosion of the number of top-level staff assistants available to recent Presidents was undoubtedly a major cause of White House lack of accountability which played so important a part in leading us both to Vietnam and Watergate.

For decades, Presidents have used the influence of senior members of committees dealing with the defense and foreign intelligence establishment to defuse, rather than confront, congressional power. Administration after administration systematically used sympathetic and powerful congressional figures for this purpose. Vital military or defense information was given to them on the explicit or tacit assumption that this information would be shielded from the knowledge of other members of Congress.

This practice began in World War II, when President Roosevelt informed a small group of key congressmen about the Manhattan Project, which had effectively been hidden from the Congress in various appropriations bills. Without doubt this particular instance was justified, given the secrecy required in wartime for a project of the utmost importance. But in the decades since World War II, this practice has been abused. Presidents have informed selected congressmen as a means of avoiding the charge of nonconsultation with the Congress; indeed, they have later often equated these disclosures to one or two key congressmen with congressional consultation and approval. Yet this is obviously neither. And the sometimes ineffective congressional oversight on such sensitive areas as intelligence and defense in recent years confirms the dangers of failing to require adequate congressional consultation and approval.

The CIA supposedly has been accountable to four House and Senate subcommittees. Yet all too often these subcommittees seemed to pay less than careful attention to this intelligence agency's activities. The former chairman of the Senate CIA Appropriations Subcommittee, for example, was asked by Senator Stuart Symington in 1971 whether the subcommittee approved funding for a 36,000-man CIA operation in Laos. The answer was astounding: "I never

119

asked to begin with whether or not there were any funds to carry on the war in the sum the CIA asked for. It never dawned on me to ask about it." And in 1966, former Senator Leverett Saltonstall, who for years was the ranking Republican member of the Senate subcommittee overseeing the CIA, typified this prevailing congressional attitude: "It is not a question of reluctance on the part of CIA officials to speak to us. Instead it is a question of our reluctance, if you will, to seek information and knowledge on subjects which I personally, as a member of Congress and as a citizen, would rather not have."

In 1971, former Congressman Richard McCarthy discovered a massive government program for the development of chemical and biological warfare technology, proving false previous military denials of the program's existence. He also discovered that senior members of the Appropriations and Armed Services Committee had known about the program. The rest of the Congress had never been informed.

The bombing of Cambodia in 1969 was hidden from the Congress by a system of false reporting that circumvented the normal chains of command within the Defense Department and the normal channels of communication between the executive branch and the appropriate congressional committees. Neither branch of Congress was formally advised of the bombing prior to May 1970. Yet a few members of Congress in positions of particular responsibility had known about the bombings earlier. The rest of the Congress was not informed.

The executive used this technique repeatedly. But the constitutional and statutory requirements for congressional consultation and approval cannot be met through private and informal consultation with a few selected congressmen. Undoubtedly, such limited consultation places those members of Congress involved in a difficult position, in which their prestige is being used as a shield from further congressional review. Article I of the Constitution, however, clearly states that "no money shall be drawn from the Treasury, but on Consequence of Appropriations made by Law; and a regular Statement and Account of the Receipts and Expenditures of all public Money shall be published from time to time." In other words, taxpayers' money cannot be spent without a congressional appropriation, and appropriations must be public. The Congress as a whole must decide when money will be spent abroad, or when war will be waged. And without stiff congressional resistance to the tactic of limited private consultation, the Congress's responsibility to play a meaningful role in the formulation of foreign policy and national security policy never will be fully realized.

The executive-legislative imbalance the nation faced by the latter years of the first Nixon administration meant the absence of effective restraint by the Congress in many spheres of Presidential conduct. Particularly in the area of foreign affairs, Presidents could avoid accountability simply because they did not perceive Congress to be a group of peers to whom they would be responsible for their actions. Indeed, recent Presidents often seem to have viewed Congress as a body to be outwitted or outflanked rather than respected and consulted. And the ease with which Congress often was outwitted and outflanked lessened respect for Congress as a body and emboldened Presidents to undertake even more irresponsible Presidential actions.

This state of affairs certainly had never been intended by the framers of the Constitution, fearful as they were of excesses in either executive or legislative power. Yet it had happened over a period of decades, acquiring a momentum that was exploited by Presidents eager for greater power and barely slowed by those seemingly committed to a greater congressional role.

Many forces were involved in this dangerous Presidential ascendancy. Three assumed particular importance: the change in America's basic domestic and international position following World War II, new and powerful communications tools and discretionary funds available to the President, and a congressional structure that sometimes failed to stop forceful Presidents from imposing their wills on the legislative branch. Each helped to weaken the restraints on accountable Presidential power; each interacted with the others to magnify a President's ability to reduce or eliminate his responsibility to the Congress.

The stage was set for the increase of Presidential power and the decline of congressional influence with the change in America's international role following World War II. Entering the postwar era as unquestioned leader of the free world and sole possessor of nuclear destruction, the United States seemed irrevocably committed to a continuing and vast role in world affairs. The evolution of a bipartisan foreign policy, seen as needed to meet the threat of communism and the newly acquired Soviet nuclear capability, turned our enlarged international role into an enlarged Presidential role. And the secrecy system that grew up around the newly perceived menace of communism gave rise to a monopoly of executive branch information that remained virtually untouched by the Congress for almost two decades. These developments provided a convenient excuse for the expansion of Presidential power abroad and curtailment of congressional oversight of that power at home.

Undergirding the credibility of Presidential leadership was the pervasive attitude that his advice was the product of such impressive intelligence, experience and information that it should be assumed to be superior to any other advice. Those who made up the "best and the brightest" dazzled America with their competence and brilliance. The establishment in the White House, the Defense Department, the State Department, the CIA and other branches of our nation's foreign policy apparatus convinced many—including myself—that the war in Vietnam was being handled by individuals with far more experience and understanding, who possessed far greater information (most of it classified), and who were thus capable of making far better judgments on those matters than the Congress, or, indeed, the American people. Because of this widely held view, Presidential judgments in foreign relations were accorded great credibility.

We now realize that the decisions affecting the war in Indochina were often flawed with error and illusion and often devoid of human understanding and compassion. Hopefully, these developments have taught us a crucial lesson: Presidential judgments must be tested by the normal standards of reason and by their acceptability to a fully informed public. They should carry no mystery.

The changes in America's world role over the past thirty years have been no greater than the changes in the nature of our society at home. And many of these changes also served to enhance Presidential power, particularly when this power was not seriously challenged by an often lethargic Congress. Of particular importance was the increasingly complex nature of the American economy, which resulted in the delegation of ever greater powers to Presidents. This trend culminated in the Economic Stabilization Act of 1970, in which the Congress gave to President Nixon vast powers over the management of the nation's economy, with only very limited controls over the exercise of those powers. Because of this legislation, the Nixon administration was able to institute and administer wage and price controls unfairly and inequitably in an effort to undermine the continuation of any controls system.

In addition to the very basic changes in our position abroad and in our society at home, the decline of congressional power and influence was aided by powerful new tools available to Presidents in their efforts to sway public opinion.

The television revolution has played a most important role in providing Presidents with an unbelievably powerful capacity to dominate telecommunications and control public discussion. Presidents have preempted this most powerful communications tool, and Congress has failed to provide an effective response to the use of television by our Presidents. The domination by recent Presidents of the national media thereby made the maintenance of other healthy institutional voices within our society more and more difficult.

And with the expansion of federal governmental power came a similar increase in the availability of discretionary monies, many new appointments to important positions, and a proliferation of the many other ways of dispensing Presidential and executive branch influence. The billions of dollars available to dispense or withhold government largesse —totally within the boundaries of legal conduct—cannot be overlooked as another important source for combatting congressional power. Often, these tools have been used as

125

effectively by the bureaucracy as by the White House; indeed, recent Presidents and their staffs have sometimes been frustrated by the ability of executive branch agencies to retain control over many of the opportunities for rewarding friends and punishing enemies that an expanding government has created.

Finally, the nature of Congress itself has helped shift the balance of accumulated power toward the Presidency and away from the legislative branch. The slowness of the congressional pace, the willingness of many to regard an ever-stronger Presidency as necessary in an age of unfamiliar challenges, and Congress's lack of new technology available to the executive branch all helped contribute to a dangerous imbalance of power.

Congress had no substantial technological assessment capability or computer technology available to it until very recently. Faced with an executive branch armed with more than seven thousand computers manned by more than fifty thousand people, at a cost of more than $2.7 billion a year, Congress even now labors along with twelve computers and fewer than five hundred people to run them.

Using these massive resources, the executive often overwhelmed Congress through its own presentations and by helping those in Congress favoring an administration position. I recall hearings on legislation dealing with multi-billion-dollar education programs where we asked the executive for computer assistance. We received either no help at all or information that was often useless. But congressional backers of administration positions received full and very valuable support as well as computer assistance.

And all too often Congress impeded its own effectiveness through the slowness of its proceedings.

The Senate filibuster rule has been particularly important in slowing down the effectiveness of Congress. From 1917 through 1974, there were 100 record cloture votes in the Senate; only 20 resulted in the end of the filibuster. And those record cloture votes tell only part of the story of defeat and delay created by the filibuster rule.

Dozens of filibusters took place during this fifty-eight-year period that did not culminate in record cloture votes. Yet their toll was surely high in terms of the defeat, the delay and the compromising of important legislation. Many bills, for instance, have been talked to death because of what they did—or did not—contain.

Similarly, bare cloture vote statistics do not reveal the bills that have been lost in the jam created by filibusters.

And just the *threat* of the filibuster, while impossible to measure, often has been as effective as an actual filibuster in influencing the legislative process.

Filibusters have delayed and blocked legislation. They have prevented the organization of the Senate, delayed the election of its officers, and blocked Presidential appointments. They also have resulted in the modification of the terms of legislation and have achieved the enactment of legislation favored by those leading the filibuster. They have delayed the adjournment of Congress and have forced special sessions. They have cost the taxpayers much money and the legislative process much time.

In the 93rd Congress alone, the filibuster left a trail of defeat, delay and compromise.

In the spring of 1973, the Senate began consideration of an efficient and effective means for registering voters. Few could dispute the basic, democratic virtue of broad voter participation. A bill came before the Senate which promised to accomplish that important goal.

Intermittently, for an entire month, we were prevented from dealing with this measure. Even though an overwhelming majority of the members of the Senate favored the pending measure, a small group of senators were able to block a vote on the bill by using the filibuster rule.

Eventually, a two-thirds vote was obtained and the filibuster was ended. But this body lost valuable legislative time, and action on an important measure was delayed.

Twice during the 93rd Congress bills came to the floor of the Senate that were aimed at reforming our system of financing political campaigns. It is important to put this legislation in context. Throughout 1973 and 1974, the American people were exposed to daily revelations of scandal at the highest levels of the executive branch of government. Public confidence in government—all branches of government—was sinking to all-time low levels. The American people clamored for action.

Twice the Senate debated important bills aimed at dealing with the root of much of the political evil the American people rebelled against—money in politics. Twice a small group of Senators frustrated the will of the Senate and the will of the American people.

In December of 1973, and again in April of 1974, we stood helpless. For a total of almost three weeks, a small group of senators inflicted legislative paralysis on the Senate.

Finally, on April 9, 1974, cloture was invoked and a campaign finance reform bill passed the Senate. But, again, the filibuster rule had taken its toll. The bill had been weakened, the Senate had lost valuable legislative time, and the American people had wondered if the Senate could really act— even in the face of the greatest political scandal in American history.

Moreover, it no longer could be said that the filibuster was the exclusive tool of the representatives of one section of the country or of one political philosophy or that it was used solely against one category of legislation—civil rights. It has been used by senators from all parts of the country and of all political philosophies.

In early 1975, we were faced with the prospect of a "filibuster Congress." The filibuster rule then in force required two-thirds of those present and voting to cut off debate on any issue. A small group of determined senators could have blocked passage of measure after measure, and the American people's faith in the ability of Congress to meet their real problems would have been further eroded.

Realizing this gloomy prospect, Senator James Pearson of Kansas and I launched a drive to reform the filibuster rule. We pointed out that from 1789 until 1806, only a majority of the Senate was needed to close off debate on legislation. And while we were not attempting to return to the days of majority cloture, we reminded the Senate that one Senate cannot bind another, and that the filibuster rule in effect as this struggle began could be changed by any succeeding Congress.

Our appeal was not to the rules of the Senate. It was to the Constitution of the United States—Article I, Section 5, which gives each House of the Congress the power to "determine the Rules of its Proceedings." What we wanted was simple: a change from two-thirds of those present and voting to three-fifths of those present and voting as the requirement for ending debate. While we did not succeed in getting this particular change, we did reduce the number of votes required to end a filibuster to a flat 60. Through this change, we took much of the potential for unnecessary delay out of the filibuster. And over time, Congress will become more effective as a result.

✽　　✽　　✽

The decline of congressional power and the rise of a dominant Presidency was the combination of complex factors. These did not spring forth suddenly on January 20, 1969, when Richard Nixon took office. They were the products in part of powerful trends in the nation, the growing complexity of problems, and the willingness of the executive to arrogate power in the face of a sometimes ineffective Congress.

The strategy of the Nixon administration was clear both in the areas of the war-making power and the congressional power of the purse. It was to rule the nation by veto—by the one-third of the Congress needed to prevent the overriding of those vetoes. If the President wanted to start an illegal war, he did so, secure in the knowledge that only two-thirds of the entire Congress could effectively blunt his actions. If the Congress appropriated funds for a program and he illegally impounded them, the only remedy was to pass legislation which required their expenditure, legislation which itself could be vetoed.

Such a strategy, of course, is within the rights of any President—indeed, it is guaranteed to him by the Constitution. But a resort to illegality is not so guaranteed. And when the line between policy disagreement and illegal action had been crossed, the Congress had the duty to respond vigorously.

We also had the ability to do so. Faced with massive

131

illegality, the Congress could have counterimpounded funds —funds for the Defense Department, funds for the White House itself, funds for the State Department. Unlike the Nixon two-thirds strategy, this congressional counterimpoundment strategy could have worked with a majority of both Houses. In order to stop appropriation of funds, only a majority is needed to carry out the congressional will. We could have done this, but we did not.

And we could have undertaken more vigorous oversight of the executive branch. We saw many of the trends which were leading to the accumulation of unaccountable power in the Nixon White House. We saw the Cabinet officers lose prestige and influence, with their powers seized by anonymous men inside the White House. We saw this, and we should have acted before a Watergate forced us to do so. But we did not.

But the nature of the American society and the unwillingness of Congress to act as forcefully as was sometimes necessary do not totally explain the decline in the accountability of government which reached its peak in the Nixon years. The Congress was not only neglectful in its pursuit of its powers. All too often, we were deceived by the executive in ways which even the most effective oversight could not have remedied. The invasion of Cambodia, the "tilt" toward Pakistan, the use of CIA funds to intervene in the political affairs of Chile—all were the results of secrecy and deception on the part of an administration willing to use illegality or unethical conduct to reach its ends.

A reluctant Congress, temporarily overwhelmed by an arrogant, immoral Nixon administration, led to a crisis of government perhaps unparalleled in our history. Watergate came as an indication of what the psychology of unrestrainable power could yield.

6

The President
and Congress

A Renaissance of
Power?

We have a system that was shrewdly designed to be strong enough for leadership, but in which power was diffuse enough to assure liberty.

—*James Reston*

Given the depths to which the institutional role of Congress had descended, a rebirth of congressional responsibility probably was inevitable. But such a renaissance might have been delayed for years had the Nixon administration not pushed so far and so fast. For ironically, its actions, totally transgressing the constitutional limitations of the Presidential office, produced a reaction that energized the Congress into fulfilling its role as a coequal branch of government far more vigorously.

134

A Renaissance of Power?

The secret bombing and later invasion of Cambodia, the massive impoundment of funds undercutting Congress's power of the purse, and the expanded use of so-called executive agreements to avoid congressional ratification represented a massive insult to the institutional prerogatives of the legislative branch. So too did the establishment of powerful offices such as the Domestic Council and the Office of Management and Budget with no accountability to the Congress, the use of theories of "executive privilege" and "national security" as tools of secrecy and obfuscation, and outright deceit and lawlessness. And while the attack on congressional prerogatives was undoubtedly begun well before Richard Nixon and his men took office, the speed and arrogance they gave to it and the deceit and illegality they used forced a response even from a reluctant Congress.

In reaction to this challenge, Congress has initiated a spate of legislative activity to reclaim many of the prerogatives it had lost over previous decades by Presidential expansion and congressional deference. A War Powers Act, passed over former President Nixon's veto, has provided a substantial degree of congressional control over the war-making power. A Budget Reform Act has given Congress a major role in the formation of the federal budget and control over Presidential impoundments. Now, by law, future OMB directors are subject to confirmation with the advice and consent of the Senate. Requirements for transmittal of all executive agreements to the Congress within sixty days of their coming into force have been enacted, and legislation giving Congress the power to disapprove of these agreements is under active consideration. A lawsuit in which I participated with three other Senators removed as head of the Office of Economic Opportunity a Nixon nominee whose name had not been submitted to the Senate for confirmation, thereby helping to clarify the Congress's prerogatives in the area of confirming nominations.

And legislation significantly defining and limiting the President's emergency powers is now being actively pursued in the Congress, following the report of a specially created Senate committee which revealed the incredible power Presidents possess through the existence of 470 unrepealed emergency powers statutes dating back to the 1930s.

In each instance, Congress has acted in a major way to regain powers that had been waning over the years. Each action is not without risk, but each holds the potential for reducing a President's ability to sweep the Congress aside in our exercise of the most basic constitutional rights.

The War Powers Act and the Budget Control Act provide especially good illustrations of the promise and risks inherent in this recent congressional legislative activity.

The War Powers Act marks a major turning point in the history of Presidential-congressional relations on the commitment of American troops abroad. It allows a President to commit U.S. armed forces pursuant only to a declaration of war, specific statutory authorization, or a national emergency created by an attack on the United States or its armed forces. It requires a President to report in writing to the Congress within forty-eight hours on any commitment or substantial enlargement of U.S. combat forces abroad. It also requires termination of any troop commitment within sixty days after an initial Presidential report has been submitted, unless Congress declares war, specifically authorizes continuation of the commitment, or is physically unable to convene as a result of an armed attack on the United States. An additional thirty-day period of commitment is allowed only if the President certifies to Congress that unavoidable military necessity required the continued use of American troops abroad.

President Ford acknowledged the Act's impact when he stated publicly that any reintroduction of American troops into Southeast Asia could not be accomplished without congressional approval. It is regrettable that the President authorized the evacuation of South Vietnamese nationals, a power not granted him under the War Powers Act, without obtaining congressional authorization. But it is even more important that any temptation to introduce American troops or bombing into Cambodia or South Vietnam in early 1975 to help "save" those governments was effectively removed by the War Powers Act. Without the Act, the President might have felt obliged to once again escalate American involvement and possibly once again plunge our nation into a major military involvement in Southeast Asia.

Admittedly, there are also significant problems in the legislation. It does not require the President to tell Congress of many actions which, over a period of time, may require the ultimate deployment of troops. A Presidential report must be sent to Congress only when these troops are actually engaged. Thus, the War Powers Act alone probably would not have prevented the initial escalation of American involvement in Vietnam, since the President could have proceeded with armed intervention after the Gulf of Tonkin incident, relying on his claim that American ships had been fired upon. Some also have argued that by legitimizing the conduct of "Presidential wars" for up to ninety days the Act fails to respond sufficiently to the Presidential challenge to the Congress's war-making power presented by recent events.

On balance, however, the War Powers Act is an important step in the Congress's drive to reassert its coordinate powers over the basic decisions affecting the course of our nation. Its long-term success will depend in good part on Congress's desire to enforce greater respect of the law by Presidents in their handling of the nation's foreign commitments.

The tragedy of our Southeast Asia policy has caused many of us to see the growth of Presidential power in foreign policy. But the gradual shift of institutional authority from

Congress to the executive branch over the past twenty years has been broader and more fundamental than many realize.

I have long believed that congressional power over spending is the cornerstone of the constitutional balance between Congress and the President. The President must have congressional approval for the funds he wants—and this means he must be willing to negotiate, to respond to some extent to congressional wishes. Presidents often sought to limit the need for these negotiations through the practice of impoundment. For at least two decades, minor impoundments had been tolerated as a management tool—perhaps not quite legal, but easier than asking for full congressional action to repeal or modify an appropriation where real disagreement did not appear to exist.

But a wave of $18 billion in impoundments announced by the Nixon administration in the spring of 1973 clearly brought home the fact that the practice of impoundment had gradually grown into a major vehicle for Presidential disregard of congressional policies embodied in legislation which the President himself had signed.

It is clear enough that one reason for the abuse of executive power was the Congress's failure to fully live up to its own responsibilities to establish budget policy. And so it was crucially important that the Congress not only limit executive impoundments but also equip itself to do a better job of overseeing its own budget decisions.

The Budget and Impoundment Control Act, enacted in the fall of 1974, does both.

The Act sets firm statutory limits once and for all on Presidential impoundments, permits veto by either House of Congress of Presidential decisions to "defer" or delay the spending of appropriated funds for a period of time, and requires approval by both Houses of Congress of Presidential requests to eliminate or "rescind" a funding item entirely.

Just as important, the new Act establishes budget committees in both the House and the Senate, and procedures which will enable the Congress to adopt, and live within, its own overall budget. I am privileged to serve on the Senate Budget Committee, and my impression is that both the House and Senate Committees have done a remarkable job in equipping themselves with able staff. A Budget Resolution, setting targets for spending revenues and debt for the fiscal year beginning July 1, 1975, has been adopted. And the new process shows every sign of creating a structure for thorough congressional discussion and determination of key economic and program choices each year.

In addition, the Act establishes a new congressional Office of the Budget to serve the Congress much as the Office of Management and Budget serves the executive branch. This office, which is now acquiring the staff of budget experts, economists and social scientists and the computer technology needed to successfully analyze the vast scope of federal activity, will in future years be the cornerstone of an increasingly sophisticated congressional budget process.

Legislators are by and large closer to the needs of their constituents than Cabinet officers or Presidents. We have, I think, a unique perspective on the way federal programs and policies work in the communities we serve. If we succeed in coupling this special insight with the kind of expertise which in the past has been available only to the executive branch, I hope and believe that this legislative-based budget process can begin to ask the hardest of all questions that can be asked about each federal program: Does it really meet the needs of those it was intended to serve? And the result will be a far more efficient and responsive federal establishment.

There are risks as well as great promise in this legislation. Efforts to establish a congressional budget process in the Legislative Reorganization Act of 1946 failed miserably because the Congress set unrealistically low spending targets and then proceeded to ignore them. Within two years, the process was abandoned. This could happen again if we do not make the Budget Control Act work in a way that truly asserts our rights to help determine priorities in government spending. Should we fail, much of Congress's power over the purse may be lost irretrievably. But success will result in a major shift in power from Presidents to Congresses in the exercise of one of Congress's most important constitutional powers. Once again, the institutional change has given us the

141

opportunity to regain lost power. But only through strong will can we make that opportunity a reality.

Virtually every other measure recently passed by Congress in its drive to reassert a degree of authority over government contains a similar potential for success or failure. Yet despite the problems, recent attempts by Congress to revive its powers have been valuable, both for the substantive limitations they have placed on Presidential conduct and for the way they have made it clear that Congress's days as a doormat are over. We have begun to inform our Chief Executives that they must involve Congress in those actions that are rightfully our joint responsibility and respect our powers in those areas which are our sole responsibility. This new relationship need not and should not undermine the legitimate powers of the Presidency. It must, however, keep those powers within the boundaries of the law and the Constitution. And it should help Presidents respect the procedures and balances of our democracy, while not lessening their ability to govern the nation.

We have begun to correct the imbalance that had endangered the effective accountability of American government. But dangers and challenges do remain.

The dangers lie in both overreaction and complacency. If Congress perceives the accumulation of power by recent Presidents as a pretext for placing unrealistically tight and restrictive checks on Presidential actions, we will be disregarding the clear necessity for effective executive leadership. Our Chief Executive must remain powerful, not transformed into a Gulliver tied down by a thousand ropes of congressional making. Indeed, enactment of substantive checks on legitimate Presidential power likely would leave the nation ungoverned and ungovernable. At the same time, Congress must avoid the notion that the substantive reforms we have already enacted will be sufficient to curb future arbitrary Presidential actions and that no more need be done in the drive to reassert Congressional authority and responsibility.

Either overreaction or complacency would be dangerous. Instead, we must begin to shift the focus of our efforts in ways that will help shape the *long-term* likelihood of a strong yet accountable Presidency and a respected and responsible Congress.

We face at least two challenges. First, we must strengthen Congress's commitment to exercise its oversight function, without which the substantive reforms already enacted may become meaningless. Second, we must ensure that, when new substantive grants of power *are* made to Presidents, sufficient procedural controls are attached to guard against abuse.

The importance of the oversight function cannot be overestimated. As Woodrow Wilson observed: "Quite as important as legislation is vigilant oversight of administration, and even more important than legislation is the instruction and guidance in political affairs which the people might receive from a body which kept all national concerns suffused in a broad daylight of discussion. The informing function of Congress should be preferred even to its legislative function."

Congressional oversight is probably the single most important component of this "informing function." And its effectiveness has been shown through the work of the Senate Watergate Committee, which forced public disclosure of the plan devised by the Nixon administration to degrade our freedoms. The power that this type of oversight possesses is amply shown by the fear the Nixon White House had of the Watergate Committee when it was first established. The Nixon tapes show this fear and reveal the great deal of work which was done to attempt to pack the committee with favorable senators and to deny it the information needed to get the job done. Yet attempts to thwart the work of the committee failed, and through its efforts the American public saw that the illegal activities undertaken by the Nixon White House were more than "just politics."

Gallup polls taken in 1973 show the shift in public opinion the committee achieved. In April of that year, only 31 percent of those polled saw Watergate as a "very serious matter," as opposed to 53 percent who regarded it as "just politics." By mid-July, after two months of committee hearings, 48 percent felt it was serious, and 45 dismissed it as ordinary politics.

The committee held the nation's attention for weeks,

helped educate us to the dangers we faced, and changed the course of American history.

We must continue to strengthen this informing function, as was done with the establishment by the Senate and House of investigatory committees to review possible illegal CIA, FBI and other intelligence agency activity at home and abroad. These committees give us another opportunity: not to tear down agencies, the legitimate exercise of whose powers is important for the security of the United States, but to help ensure that their activities remain within the law and subject to continuing congressional oversight.

The congressional legislative committees also must begin a much delayed but greatly needed review of the entire range of our domestic programs. For too long we have not performed aggressively enough the tough, sometimes tedious job of determining the effectiveness of our programs in such areas as health, education, housing and transportation. This failure has enabled recent administrations to terminate programs they claimed were ineffective without sufficient congressional input into the decision-making process. The Nixon administration's sudden decision in 1973 to end many federal housing subsidy programs is an excellent example of this kind of arrogance. But it is also the partial result of a Congress that failed to monitor and oversee the effectiveness of those same housing programs. Had we done so, it would have been more difficult for the administration to undertake what they did.

A change in outlook is needed within the Congress. It will

be difficult to achieve such a shift in a body that often prefers legislation to oversight, but the change is necessary if the reforms we legislate are to have real meaning and if we are to secure a long-term sense of Presidential concern with the consequences of their actions. It is essential to the restoration of public confidence.

This concern should be at the heart of Presidential actions, for as Thomas Jefferson once remarked, "Whenever you are to do a thing, though it can never be known but to yourself, ask yourself how you would act were all the world looking at you, and act accordingly." Vigorous congressional oversight will help ensure a Presidential awareness that anticipates the certainty of thorough congressional scrutiny.

While a fundamental change in congressional attitude toward the oversight function is of primary importance, reform of some congressional institutional arrangements is also essential. A number of changes should be included. Establishment of an Office of Congressional Legal Counsel would give Congress an "in-house" capacity to sue the executive branch to protect against usurpation of congressional powers. The need for such an office has become obvious in recent years as congressmen have tried on their own to halt illegal executive branch activity through the courts.

Early in 1973, for instance, twenty-two senators and five representatives helped challenge the legality of the Department of Transportation's impoundment of funds for road construction in the state of Missouri. Winning the case established a valuable precedent in restricting Presidential impoundments.

In 1972, thirteen House members sought an injunction against prosecution of the war in Indochina unless Congress authorized the war within sixty days. The case was unsuccessful but it brought the issue of congressional war powers to the public eye. Other suits brought by a number of members of Congress over the years have sought access to information under the Freedom of Information Act. Again, while many of these cases were unsuccessful, they have been valuable in bringing to the public's attention the problems inherent in government secrecy.

These suits—and many others brought by members of Congress—were handled by private lawyers. These attorneys performed magnificently, but the Congress should not be completely reliant on the goodwill of private resources.

Creation of an office of Congressional Legal Counsel, as I have proposed in legislation, would give Congress ongoing oversight through the courts and thereby help make more meaningful the substantive reforms we have enacted and will enact. Hopefully, these reforms will redefine executive and legislative branch prerogatives and powers, making frequent use of legal action unnecessary. But Congress still must have the means to obtain enforcement of the laws it passes and its powers under the Constitution.

This counsel, for example, could help enforce congressional rights under the Freedom of Information Act. In the past, overclassification of documents has been a major shield used by the executive to avoid accountability to the Congress. Recent changes in the Freedom of Information Act will make it easier to obtain this type of information, and while legal action hopefully will not be necessary, if it is, the Congressional Legal Counsel would be available to help.

To complement the Office of Legal Counsel, I believe we need a question-and-report period along the lines of parliamentary practice. At present, key executive branch officials do come to the Congress, but their testimony is given before committees, not before an entire body. And yet every member of the Senate has a strong interest in the major issues facing the Congress. I have sponsored legislation that would help us explore these interests by establishing a question-and-report period, available to all media, including live radio and television, during which appropriate Cabinet and other executive department officials would present themselves for questions before the full Senate and answer all questions posed by senators.

This is not a new or radical idea. In 1864, a select committee of the House, and in 1881, a select committee of the Senate recommended the right of the floor of both Houses to Cabinet officers to answer questions and participate in debate. In 1912, President Taft, in a message to Congress, made virtually the same recommendation. And throughout the 1940s and 1950s, Senator Estes Kefauver received widespread public support for his advocacy of a question-and-report period, with a 1943 Gallup poll showing 72 percent in favor and only 7 percent opposed to the idea.

I recently watched a question period during a session of the Canadian Parliament and came away even more convinced of the validity of the process. Since we do not have a Parliamentary system, it may not work quite as satisfactorily for us. But there were several features of the Canadian question period which struck me as being very important and which I believe would maintain much of their importance even if transplanted into our nonparliamentary system.

The Canadian Cabinet officers were dealt with not as superior public officials deserving special deference but simply as coequals who deserved only such respect as they earned. In our system, Cabinet officers are not members of the legislative branch, as they are in parliamentary countries, and perhaps because of that a mystique has been built up which accords Cabinet officers a special status that interferes with candid communications. The tradition, the perquisites of office, the pay—all have contributed to this special status. Hopefully, a procedure involving a no-holds barred question period would help create a more democratic attitude and approach on the part of Cabinet officers and other executive branch officials.

I was told by very high officials in the Canadian Parliament that the question period was of great assistance to members of government because they could quickly see which of their Cabinet officers were unable to answer questions put to them on an intelligent and effective basis, and they could then make changes before that Cabinet official got them into more trouble. And also they told me that through this institution they could spot policy errors and mistakes much sooner. If a Cabinet officer begins to duck or evade a question, it becomes immediately obvious to the Parliament, to his fellow Cabinet officers, and to the Prime Minister. And if there is a fundamental weakness in an official policy, it is understood that it must be quickly corrected or further embarrassment was unavoidable. One Canadian official told me that it was always his opinion that if we had had a question-and-report period in Congress, the war in Vietnam—because of its indefensibility—might have ended much earlier.

I also believe that the question-and-report period proposal should be tried because it could well strengthen the Cabinet as a part of the executive branch and result in the appointment of stronger Cabinet officials. If a President knows that Cabinet officers are going to be subject to this kind of searching public questioning and are going to be held accountable for the policies and the practices of their departments, I believe there will be a growing trend to pick stronger Cabinet officers who can stand up to this challenge in support of the administration.

And I believe there would be a tendency to provide Cabinet officers with more authority to make decisions. To appoint a Secretary to head a department without providing that person with appropriate authority would place that officer in an untenable position, which would quickly become obvious under the pressure of the questioning from the Congress. I suspect that men and women of stature would not agree to be put in that position. They would require as a condition of accepting a nomination to a Cabinet position an agreement that they would have greater authority over their departments.

As Arthur Schlesinger, Jr., has observed, such a question-and-report period might have "quite extensive consequences for the traditional system":

> As for the President, a question hour could subtly alter the balance of his personal power both as against his Cabinet, whose members would have the chance to acquire new visibility and develop their own relationships with Congress and the electorate, and as Congress, which would have the opportunity of playing off his own cabinet against him.

It is an experiment well worth undertaking.

A similar need exists for more scrutiny of the Executive Office of the President. Specifically, we need legislation establishing a statutory basis for key White House office jobs, which came close to enactment in 1974. Such legislation would give Congress the basis for holding hearings to determine the extent of White House employee influence; it would also allow Congress to investigate the possible need for further cutbacks in top White House staff positions to help assure greater Cabinet department accountability.

We should bolster this legislation with the requirement that heads of the Domestic Council and the National Security Council be subject to Senate confirmation. Clearly, our principal means of increasing responsibility within the executive branch must be to bring more authority back to the Cabinet departments. But confirmation of additional key White House aides—similar to the confirmation of the heads of the Office of Management and Budget and the Council on International Economic Policy now written into law—would give Congress a greater ability to probe the activities and attitudes of the principal advisors within the White House. This ability also could be enhanced by creating permanent oversight subcommittees in the Government Operations committees of both the House and Senate. These subcommittees would monitor the size, nature and activites of the Executive Office of the President, where so much unaccountable power has accumulated.

Greater use must be made of fresh, specially created select and temporary committees to conduct intensive oversight of particularly important national policy areas. Given broad mandates and a fixed time for existence, committees of this type can take a global focus on problems of particular importance. In the past, the Senate has created effective select or temporary committees to probe key policy areas and recommend reforms. One such committee has effectively documented the problems of hunger and malnutrition in America, and has helped move us toward a more humane food policy. Another revealed the existence of 470 unrepealed emergency powers, statutes which gave Presidents virtually dictatorial powers, should they choose to invoke them. As a result of this committee's work, legislation repealing these statutes and substituting a joint Presidential-congressional procedure for new grants of emergency powers is now actively being pursued in the Congress. And the Select Committee on Equal Educational Opportunity, which I chaired for almost three years, did valuable work in analyzing the nation's desperate need for more effective educational opportunities for the nation's children, particularly children of the poor.

The record of these and other such committees should prompt the Congress to use them more frequently. The failure of the committees charged with oversight of our nation's intelligence agencies and in particular the CIA and FBI—may well have played an important part in permitting questionable domestic and foreign intelligence activities to occur. And the creation of a select committee on intelligence activities has thereby helped begin the process of restoring the nation's confidence in the propriety of these agencies' operations. These bodies can bring a freshness of approach which can help examine the failures of past performance and recommend ways of doing better in the future. And they can allow new senators and congressmen the opportunity to spend time on these important questions, time which others in the Congress are sometimes unable to invest. Democratic Majority Leader Mike Mansfield is to be commended for his appointment of two freshmen Democratic senators to the Senate select committee on intelligence operations. They have brought strength to this vital committee and have helped all of us on the committee deal with very difficult questions.

None of these institutional changes will succeed, of course, without congressional willingness to use them aggressively. Success will require a desire to undertake much day-to-day work that is less dramatic and more tedious than many aspects of the legislative process. But unless we are willing to probe, to inquire, to insist on greater monitoring of the executive branch's performance, all the well-drafted legislation we pass to assure executive accountability could be fruitless.

In the past we have paid dearly for this lack of adequate congressional oversight. If we had pursued more vigorously the web of regional commitments and obligations in which we were being enmeshed in Southeast Asia, there is at least a chance that Vietnam would not have become a national tragedy. If we had been more vigorous in watching the expansion of the White House staff and the operations of the CIA and the FBI, we might have prevented the temptations that led to the worst excesses of Watergate.

And had we done a better job in our scrutiny of the many domestic social programs passed in the 1960s, it would have helped us to get our money's worth and to ensure that these programs were working as planned.

Hopefully, the new Senate Budget Committee will provide the type of sophisticated program evaluation which we have only rarely done in the Congress. I believe that other committees dealing with education, health, the environment or housing should set aside 1 or 2 percent of a program's funding for a truly independent evaluation of their effectiveness. And we should encourage the use of "zero budgeting," in which we completely reexamine the effectiveness of all programs before funding them anew. These techniques could save taxpayers' money and make our domestic programs more effective. And when Americans are persuaded that their tax dollars are being well spent, public confidence in these essential programs will increase.

To make our oversight power more effective, we must be willing to force executive branch compliance. A review of the government classification system that enables so much defense and foreign-policy–related information to escape congressional examination is imperative. More liberal use of our subpoena powers to force the appearance of witnesses and the production of important documentation would help. And we should establish a permanent office of public attorney to help the Congress deal with corruption or conflict of interest within the executive branch.

Strengthening Congress's oversight functions has the great benefit of flexibility, since those functions can be used in a variety of ways and in a multitude of changing circumstances. And ensuring that this oversight responsibility is continually and effectively exercised will be a potent congressional weapon in reestablishing a system of restraints on unaccountable Presidential actions and a sense of greater Presidential obedience to the law and awareness of the constitutional position of the Congress.

As important as it is to strengthen congressional oversight, other action obviously will be needed to restore congressional prerogatives. Congress will be required not only to oversee the executive but also to take the initiative in many substantive areas of governmental responsibility.

By reducing the power of an intransigent minority to tie up the Senate when it is considering vital legislation, the change in the Senate filibuster rule should make it easier for Congress to initiate, evaluate, and pass its own programs. The will of the Senate, and the will of the American people, will be able to be better translated into legislative programs.

It is important to note, however, that under this reform the rights of the minority are still given extensive protection.

The essential character of the Senate, as one of the most significant and powerful deliberative bodies in the world, had not been destroyed. There will still be time for careful and thoughtful consideration and deliberation. Cloture will still be difficult to obtain. Legislation will remain the product of extensive examination. But I am confident that this change will permit the Congress to act more swiftly on essential legislation in the fields of tax reform, consumer protection, energy policy, health care, and other areas of current concern. We have already seen the effect of this change in aiding the repeal of the oil depletion allowance in early 1975, a long-overdue change that might not have been possible had the old filibuster rule been in effect.

We must recognize, however, that positive congressional action will often involve continued delegations of authority to the executive branch. It would be fruitless and probably destructive (and often unconstitutional) for the Congress to attempt to undertake executive functions. Congress cannot carry out the laws nor provide symbolic national leadership, for the simple reason that a nation with a collective leadership of 535 could not function. Yet recognition of the need for executive leadership need not blind us to the potential for congressional leadership in ways best suited to Congress's structure. Nor should it hamper essential congressional delegation of authority to the executive. But we must do so with great care and with as much specificity as a particular area will allow. Then we must monitor implementation vigorously to ensure that the executive has not subverted the legislative intent.

Congress will do this job better if vigorous oversight is coupled with a longer period of legislative authorization for federal programs. At present, for example, we no sooner pass an extension of the Elementary and Secondary Education Act than we begin hearings on the next extension of the program. This is the case with most domestic programs, which are enacted for short periods of from two to four years. Too often, this takes away time and attention from conducting really thoroughgoing oversight of specifics. How, for example, is the executive implementing Title I, which is so vital in aiding millions of poor American children? If we extended programs like these for longer periods, simply amending them as we go along, it would give us more time to concentrate on the oversight and appropriations processes and thus exert more influence over the legislation.

Another important way to avoid either too much specificity or generality in legislation is through use of the legislative veto.

Through this device, Congress can give the President a basic authority he needs while ensuring that it can take a close look at the specifics of a Presidential action or authority. There are a number of variations on the legislative veto. Basically, it involves insertion into a statute by the Congress of requirements that actions contemplated by the executive cannot become effective or cannot continue until Congress has been notified and given a specified period of time in which to approve or disapprove them. Until recently it had been used primarily in dealing with plans to reorganize the executive branch of the government. In 1973 and 1974, it was incorporated in three major pieces of legislation—the War Powers Act, the Budget Control Act and the Trade Reform Act—as a means of dividing power between the two branches.

We simply must use this device more frequently. Congress could have used it to block the Reorganization Plan that created the Domestic Council and the Office of Management and Budget in 1970. But we failed to understand the implications of the proposal and didn't employ the check that we had provided.

Use of specific congressionally mandated triggering standards as the condition for Presidential action is another means of curtailing arbitrary Presidential action without eliminating that ability to act where necessary. The President's power in dealing with the economy may be an area where this kind of action might work well. In the past, Congress has delegated too much of the vast power that our Presidents have over the economy without adequate control over its use. Still, many have recognized the need for Presidential authority to respond quickly to changing economic conditions.

Giving the President *carte blanche* to do so would be counterproductive. It might make quick action possible, but it would probably also result in unaccountable action. Congress can recognize the executive need to respond more quickly to changing economic conditions and yet limit the possibility of arbitrary action. One proposal that has been discussed would allow the President to cut taxes by up to 5 percent and release up to $2 billion in federal employment spending when certain specified economic conditions exist, while larger changes would continue to be a congressional responsibility. Congress would define those conditions—such as a specified unemployment rate or a specified negative growth rate in the gross national product—and the President could then submit his proposed action to the Congress. If Congress did not reject the action within sixty days, it would take effect for a limited period of time and could be renewed through the same process.

As we proved in early 1975, Congress can act effectively to provide major stimulus to the economy. But we can still permit Presidents to take necessary steps while retaining in Congress the power to legislate in more sweeping fashion.

Whatever the specifics of particular proposals, Congress can safeguard grants of authority—where it believes such grants are in the public interest—to ensure that power is not abused. Failure to recognize the need for greater Presidential power in certain areas is as short-sighted and dangerous as failure to recognize the need for checking excessive Presidential powers. In either case, Congress's ability to bring about greater Presidential responsiveness to it and the law will be limited only by its collective imagination and courage.

A renaissance of power has begun on Capitol Hill. In recent months, substantial doubts have been raised concerning the strength and durability of this shift in executive-legislative relations. And certainly, recent congressional behavior dictates that we carefully analyze congressional shortcomings and strengthen our effort to keep the movement toward greater congressional responsibility alive.

We cannot yet say with certainty whether this movement can be sustained and broadened, thereby reaffirming Congress's place as partner in the decisions of American government. This partnership should neither subjugate the Presidency to the Congress nor maintain Presidential dominance over the Congress. We need strength in both the Presidency and in the Congress and an appreciation of the ways in which those strengths must interact to provide responsible government.

The attitude of the American public will be crucial in seeking this type of mutual strength. The Congress cannot reassert its powers alone. The American people must continue to feel the need for balance in government and the importance of a strong Congress as an essential part of that balance. The lessons of Watergate should be remembered —not to assess blame or to gain partisan advantage, but to warn the American people continually of the dangers that occur when one branch of our government attempts to overrun the others.

Watergate has brought a sense of awareness of these dangers to this country. It would be tragic if that awareness now faded with time and the change of Presidents. For unless institutional changes continue to make Congress more effective and unless those changes are accompanied by a long-lasting public perception of the need for a vigorous Congress, the lessons of recent years could once again be lost—and the next time we might not emerge with our constitutional system intact.

7

The Ultimate Sanction

The Presidency and the Impeachment Remedy

The right of the impeachment and of trial by the legislature is the mainspring of the great machine of government. It is the pivot on which it turns. If preserved in full vigor, and exercised with perfect integrity, every branch will perform its duty, and the people be left to the performance of theirs, in the most simple form, and with complete effect, as the sovereign power of the state.
— James Monroe, The People, The Sovereigns

Americans revere their President, and rightly they should. . . . We would strive to strengthen and protect the Presidency. But if there be no accountability, another President will feel free to do as he chooses. The next time there may be no watchman in the night.
— Representative James Mann, proceedings in the House Judiciary Committee, July 1974

When the framers of the Constitution met in 1787 to devise a document for guiding an experiment in democratic government, they drew on their experiences both as colonists and as free men. Colonists for over a century, they feared that an excess of power in the executive could lead to tyranny. As

163

free men for little more than a decade, they feared that an excess of ineffective legislative domination could lead to anarchy. The system of checks and balances they devised, in the words of Justice Brandeis, was fashioned

> not to promote efficiency but to preclude the exercise of arbitrary power. The purpose was not to avoid friction, but by means of inevitable friction incident to the distribution of the government powers among three departments, to save the people from autocracy.

By giving Congress strong institutional powers and by creating the skeleton of a national judicial system, the framers tried to establish checks that would prevent the rise of a peculiarly American autocracy. Pitting "ambition against ambition," in Madison's words, they balanced constitutional powers between the executive and legislative branches. With the Bill of Rights, they attempted to ensure basic civil liberties and the rights of a free press. And those who followed them added further constitutional protection and developed the role of the political party as another check against autocracy.

These were the keys to the balanced system of American government which has worked so well for much of our two-hundred-year history. They were the keys through which would be obtained that ultimate expression of Presidential accountability—obedience to and respect for the law.

This sytem of formal and informal institutions was to become the guardian of American liberty for which the Revolutionary War had been waged. Yet the framers of the Constitution realized their system could break down. They foresaw the likelihood of attempts to turn the carefully crafted Constitution into an instrument of domination or even tyranny. And so they tried to reduce this possibility through the use of checks on executive power and also through the nature of the executive branch itself. Indeed, one of the most vigorous and ongoing debates of the Constitutional Convention centered around whether unitary or multiple executive leadership would serve the new republic most beneficially. Resistance to the concept of a unitary Chief Executive was fierce and widespread. Men like Edmund Randolph felt it represented the "foetus of monarchy." Others, such as Madison, also had serious difficulty with the idea, preferring instead a "small number" of leaders, to make it impossible for one individual to move the nation toward monarchy.

But the work done by James Wilson, chairman of the convention's Committee on Detail, eventually led to the adoption of a single executive. Wilson felt "a principal reason for unity in the executive" was "that officers might be appointed by a single responsible person." In the end, the fear of monarchy was overcome by the desire for accountability. Alexander Hamilton described the reasoning behind this fateful choice most effectively in Federalist Paper No. 70:

> [T]he plurality of the executive tend to deprive the people of the two greatest securities they can have for the faithful exercise of any delegated power; first, the restraints of public opinion which lose their efficacy as well on account of the division of the censure attendant on bad measures among a number, as on account of the uncertainty on whom it ought to fall; and second, the opportunity of discovering with facility and clearness of the misconduct of the persons they trust, in order either to their removal from office or to their actual punishment in cases which admit of it.

An additional step was needed to make one person responsible for his decisions and the decisions of those appointed by him. Despite the restraints placed on executive action by Congress, the courts, the press, the civil liberties of the people, and the criminal law, there had to be an ultimate check on individuals who violated the trust placed in them by the public. Should all other restraints fail, and a serious abuse of public trust occur, the ultimate sanction of impeachment could be used.

Impeachment developed over hundreds of years of English practice, and there were differing views of the power and the reasons for including it in the Constitution. Nevertheless our foremost impeachment scholar, Raoul Berger, has observed that the framers' view of impeachment was influenced by the English Parliament's struggles in the seventeenth century to curb those ministers who became the tools of royalist oppression. He has observed:

> Familiarity with absolutist Stuart claims raised the spectre of a President swollen with power and grown tyrannical; and fear of presidential abuses prevailed over frequent objections that impeachment threatened his independence.

Despite the noisy protestations of Richard Nixon's defenders during his impeachment ordeal, the kinds of transgressions for which impeachment was to be invoked seem fairly clear. As Berger and most other scholars see it, English precedent did not limit use of impeachment only to indictable crimes.

The "indictable crime" or "smoking gun" theory had surfaced during the impeachment trial of Andrew Johnson. But as one senator remarked during that trial, this theory yielded the improbable result that a person in the highest public office could completely undermine the integrity and responsibility of that office and be unimpeachable, but if he stole a chicken and were caught, he could be impeached and convicted.

Such a result was clearly not the intent of the framers. Justice Story wrote in 1833 that:

> Not but that crimes of a strictly legal character fall within the scope of the power; but that it has a more enlarged operation, and reaches, what are aptly termed political offenses, growing out of personal misconduct, or gross neglect, or usurpation, or habitual disregard of the public interest in the discharge of the duties of political office.

The impeachment inquiry staff of the House Judiciary Committee concluded similarly in February 1974: "A requirement of criminality would be incompatible with the intent of the framers to provide a mechanism broad enough to maintain the integrity of constitutional government."

While the impeachment remedy should not be confined to indictable crimes, it also must not be construed to authorize removal for differences over policy. The founders did not intend that Congress should be able to express its disagreement with Presidents over policy through the mechanism of impeachment. James Madison rejected use of the term "maladministration" instead of "high crimes and misdemeanors" in the impeachment clause precisely because "so vague a term will be equivalent to a tenure during the pleasure of the Senate."

Other institutional devices—ranging from the power of the purse and the war-making power to the congressional power to override vetoes and the powers of congressional investigation and oversight—were provided to handle policy differences. Ultimately, the most basic method of resolving these differences was to be the election process. Impeachment had a different and higher purpose, which, as one senator who participated in the trial of Andrew Johnson noted, should be exercised "with extreme caution" and only in "extreme cases." This purpose was to prevent one person from destroying American democracy because he viewed the Presidential office as being removed from the ultimate control of the American people. As the House Judiciary Committee staff argued, the impeachment power was to punish the significant effects of Presidential misconduct: "undermining the integrity of office, disregard of constitutional duties and oath of office, arrogation of power, abuse of the governmental process, which has an adverse impact on the system of government." Impeachment was to be the crucial and decisive remedy to restrain the arbitrary exercise of Presidential power. It would and should be tested infrequently, but when so tested, the impeachment remedy would be required to perform successfully if democracy were to survive.

If impeachment was to be used only in the most extreme cases and with greatest caution, the misconduct of Richard Nixon's administration left many Americans wondering whether that instrument's inherent nature and years of disuse had made it unserviceable in the world of twentieth-century superpowers. In the history of the republic, only twelve impeachments had reached the Senate. Only four, all of judges, resulted in convictions.

The only other Presidential impeachment proceeding had left a profound uneasiness in the minds of many. The impeachment trial of Andrew Johnson lasted for more than two months in an age when war was waged with rifles, not missiles. It was natural to wonder whether the slow, possibly laborious impeachment of Richard Nixon was feasible in the late twentieth century.

The Johnson impeachment trial left other unfortunate and troubling legacies, for it had grown out of precisely the kind of policy dispute that the framers had not intended to be remedied through the impeachment power. As historian W.R. Brock has noted:

> When impeachment finally arrived, everyone accepted the fact that the breach [by Johnson] of the Tenure of Office Act was not the real cause of the impeachment; it was necessary to prove a specific breach of the law but the reason was the need to dem-

170

onstrate that a President could not pursue a policy rejected by the legislature.

Thaddeus Stevens expressed the same sentiment when he told the House of Representatives: "Andrew Johnson must learn he is your servant and that as Congress shall order he must obey." Had the impeachment of Andrew Johnson been successful, it might well have replaced the executive tyranny against which impeachment was designed with an equally repugnant legislative tyranny.

With this history, the nation launched into its second use of the impeachment power against a President. Ironically, the incident that touched off the first wave of impeachment sentiment in 1973—the firing of Special Prosecutor Archibald Cox—involved the same constitutional power of removal which, in a much different context, had brought about impeachment proceedings against Andrew Johnson. The difference was that Johnson's removal of Secretary of War Stanton involved Presidential violation of a statute Congress passed to ensure that its policy for Reconstruction would be obeyed. The dismissal of Special Prosecutor Cox by Richard Nixon, on the contrary, involved not a difference of policy but an attempt to cover up massive violations of law. Nixon was not motivated by a desire to keep the Presidency as a coordinate branch of government but rather by the desire to prevent his Presidency from being responsible either to an-

171

other branch of government or to the American people.

The firing of Archibald Cox was not the first disturbing act of the Nixon administration, however. By then it was all too clear that the psychology of the Nixon White House was based not on belief in the law but on a belief that there were ways around it; not on respect for the Constitution but on respect for those who could bend that document in search of some "higher" political good.

This was particularly dangerous because the Nixon White House used the most sensitive agencies as the vehicles for illegal activity. One of these agencies—the CIA—occupies one of the most sensitive and delicate positions of any agency in our government. And the others—the FBI, the IRS and the Department of Justice—are unique in American government because they have access to the intimate details of the lives of Americans.

Indeed, what most basically distinguishes our system of government from totalitarian nations is the basic premise inherent in the Bill of Rights that government cannot violate the rights of citizens to be secure from "unreasonable searches and seizures." And yet the very agencies which the Nixon administration sought to turn to illegal ends had the power to nullify this basic liberty. Having acquired power over decades and having used that power for the enforcement of the law, these agencies were now to be made instrumentalities of official lawlessness. The record of what they did is clear and frightening.

172

□ The Nixon White House used the International Revenue Service to discover damaging information about its political enemies. In September of 1972, John Dean met with then-IRS Commissioner Johnnie Walters and gave Walters a list of 490 individuals, many of whom worked on the McGovern Presidential campaign, and conveyed instructions to Walters from John Ehrlichman to develop information on these individuals. According to the report of the Senate Watergate Committee, "Dean was hopeful that the Internal Revenue Service could acquire information that was requested without creating any political problems."

Fortunately, because of Treasury Secretary George Shultz's good sense, nothing was done on this request. But other requests for tax information and income tax audits were requested by White House personnel and supplied by various IRS employees. A variety of improper activities was undertaken, ranging from White House requests to "do something" about audits then being conducted on Nixon friends Billy Graham and John Wayne to requests for audits and taxpayer information on Democratic political figures.

□ The Federal Bureau of Investigation was used to obtain derogatory information about various individuals and then leak this information to the press in an attempt to discredit them. Perhaps the most infamous case was the FBI investigation of CBS reporter Daniel Schorr which, according to John Dean, was requested by H.R. Haldeman. Schorr, who had been broadcasting what the Nixon administration considered unfriendly comments, was subjected to a "full-field wide-open investigation," undertaken with the approval of the FBI Director J. Edgar Hoover. When word of the investigation leaked to the press, the White House attempted to blunt the adverse public reaction by announcing that Schorr was being considered for a high administration post and that the FBI investigation was simply a preliminary background check. In fact, as Haldeman later admitted, Schorr was not under consideration for any job. The FBI investigation was simply an attempt to discredit and harass Schorr as one part of the administration policy of action against the news media.

In addition, the FBI was used, on authorization of the President, to install wiretaps on the home telephones of a variety of individuals beginning in the spring of 1969. These included employees of the National Security Council, employees of the White House, television and newspaper reporters, and others. It is clear that many of these wiretaps were not related to national security but rather were related to domestic political matters and were attempts to gain information on "enemies" of the administration. As the House Judiciary Committee impeachment inquiry report stated: "Evidence before the Committee shows . . . that some of the taps were not legal, that they did not concern national security, but that they were installed for political purposes, in the President's interest and behalf."

The President also authorized enlisting the aid of the CIA

in connection with the so-called plumbers operation. Howard Hunt received assistance from the CIA beginning in July of 1971, including a disguise and false identification. This assistance was used by Hunt in a variety of illegal activities, including the break-in at the office of Dr. Daniel Ellsberg's psychiatrist and at Watergate itself. Similarly, the CIA provided equipment for Gordon Liddy in connection with his involvement with the plumbers' operation. In addition, David Young requested and received from the CIA a psychological profile of Dr. Ellsberg, something which Young told CIA Director Richard Helms the President knew.

☐ The President of the United States approved the so-called Houston plan for widespread surveillance of Americans, a plan which admitted illegality on its face. The philosophy and recommendations of this document, perhaps the most frightening official document in American history, meant that the President no longer felt himself bound by the law or the Constitution. It was the first charter designed to establish a secret political police, of which the plumbers were to be the forerunners. Only the disapproval of the plan by then-FBI Director J. Edgar Hoover prevented illegal government activity on a scale frightening to contemplate and perhaps fatal to our democracy. This pattern of conduct constituted a direct attack on our system of American liberties. The most basic constitutional restraints in our system had broken down through official lawlessness.

A vigorous reaction by the institutions surrounding the President to block this attempt to remove the restraints of the law from the conduct of the Presidential office became essential. Yet there was reason to doubt that these institutions would prove capable of doing so. The media had proven their value by exposing the illegal activity which was now to culminate in the possible impeachment of a President. However, the performance of two coequal branches of American government—the Congress and the judiciary—remained to be tested. As we have seen, the Congress had begun to fight back after years of institutional lethargy. But as the Watergate saga unfolded, Americans had reason to worry not only about the ability of the Congress to react effectively but also about the willingness of the courts to help check illegal Presidential conduct and restore Presidential accountability.

Historically, the judiciary has played a passive role in restraining Presidential conduct. It was reluctant to test its powers in direct confrontations with Presidents. And the exceptions—such as the *Steel Seizure* case, for example—prove the rule in two ways: first, by the infrequency with which the courts, and particularly the Supreme Court, have sought to challenge Presidential prerogatives, and second, by the process by which the Court has implicitly left unchallenged broad definitions of Presidential power at the same time it was ostensibly striking down a particular Presidential prerogative.

In the *Steel Seizure* case, President Truman's order to the

Secretary of Commerce to seize and operate all domestic steel mills in the face of potential disruption to our supply of American troops in Korea was declared unconstitutional. But the decision was based on seven separate opinions which failed to develop a coherent theory of Presidential prerogatives in domestic affairs. Depending on which opinion is read, the restrictions placed on arbitrary Presidential action shrink or expand. And even the most brilliant of the opinions, that of Justice Jackson, outlines a theory of three-tiered divisions of Presidential and congressional prerogatives which implies only minor limitations of Presidential power based on a technical reading of the statutes.

While the *Steel Seizure* case blocked President Truman's action, it implicitly approved even wider uses of his powers. And the Court has been even more reluctant to restrain Presidents in the field of foreign affairs. In the *Curtiss Wright* case, decided in 1936, the Court declared that "fundamental differences" existed between Presidential powers in domestic affairs and those powers in foreign affairs. Presidential conduct abroad—precisely the area in which unaccountable Presidential power has grown most spectacularly—was to be construed most liberally. The Court's justifications for giving the President sweeping powers in foreign affairs—his "confidential sources of information," his knowledge of "the conditions which prevail in foreign countries"—helped establish the cult of executive expertise on which the secrecy system was established.

The long and tangled history of attempts to obtain a ruling

on the constitutionality of various aspects of our involvement in Indochina confirms the essential passivity of the courts in the war-making area. By the early 1970s, a few lower courts did rule on the question of constitutionality —and those that did rebuked the Congress for sanctioning the war through its resolutions and its appropriations. Yet even by 1973, the Supreme Court moved with unusual haste to prevent implementation of a lower court ruling declaring the bombing of Cambodia unconstitutional. The Court had once again confirmed its unwillingness to tangle with the executive branch in matters of war and peace.

It was against this background that the impeachment power was to be tested as a remedy against precisely the type of massive abuse of Presidential power and betrayal of the public trust which had led to its inclusion in the Constitution. The stakes were enormous. Upon the outcome of this proceeding would depend not only the accountability of the highest government officials for their behavior but also the integrity of vital government agencies, the constitutional requirement that the President faithfully execute the laws, and in the end the ability of the impeachment process itself to act as the ultimate restraint on unaccountable Presidential conduct. If the process failed, the precedent set for future Presidents would have been disastrous; if it succeeded, the success of the democratic experiment itself would be reaffirmed.

The essential question remained: Would the impeachment process work, or would it in the end confirm the fears of Alexander Hamilton, who wrote that the prosecution of impeachment

> will seldom fail to agitate the passions of the whole community and to divide it into parties more or less friendly or inimical to the accused. In many cases it will connect itself with the preexisting factions and in such cases there will always be the greatest danger that the decision will be regulated more by the comparative strength of the parties than by the real demonstration of innocence or guilt.

There were more than ample reasons to fear Hamilton's warning in early 1974, since the entire Presidency of Richard Nixon had been based on his ability to divide the nation. As Clayton Fritchey observed:

> Franklin Roosevelt carried all but two states by telling the people they had nothing to fear but fear itself. Richard Nixon carried all but one state by making them fear everything, especially each other. Blacks against whites, young against old, hawks against doves, AFL against CIO, educated against uneducated, fundamentalists against free thinkers.

Nixon's Presidency had become a means for postponing rather than fostering national reconciliation after the horrors of the Vietnam War. In that atmosphere the country, already divided by a national leadership that played to the people's fears, entered another potentially divisive national debate.

Thankfully, our fears did not prove justified and our sense of national unity was enhanced by the impeachment proceedings. Hamilton's warning proved to be unfounded, for although passions were aroused, they never destroyed the fundamental evenhandedness of the proceedings or their value in illuminating the abuses of Presidential power. Although there was partisanship throughout the proceedings, it ultimately became more of a unifying than a divisive factor in the nation as men and women from both parties saw the need to save our system from the abuses to which it had been subjected.

That the impeachment inquiry did not proceed to its ultimate conclusion is beside the point. By the time Richard Nixon resigned, it had laid the foundation requiring that the ultimate judgment be rendered with fairness and deliberation. Although Mr. Nixon's resignation prevented an actual impeachment by the House and his trial in the Senate, it is generally assumed that conviction in such a trial was inevitable. Indeed, the chances of his conviction were so overwhelming that pressure from his own party played a large part in his resignation. And while his own resignation statement contained no admission of guilt, it is virtually certain that he left office knowing that he was one step ahead of conviction.

In the process, we learned a host of valuable lessons both about ourselves and impeachment, and we established and reaffirmed a number of valuable principles for the future.

☐ First, the essential nature of the impeachment power itself was confirmed and further clarified. Impeachment would not be used as an instrument of congressional domination over a President who had failed to carry out its policies but rather as an instrument of the nation against a President who had abused the powers entrusted in him. Neither would it be limited to bringing judgment only for indictable crimes but rather as a means for expressing the collective desire of the nation that its Presidents remain ultimately accountable to the people, and that gross, massive violations of the public trust would be punished through removal from office.

The House Judiciary Committee considered either publicly or privately a large number of potential articles of impeachment against Richard Nixon. That the majority were never brought to a vote reflects the restraint and sense of responsibility that the House committee exhibited. That the majority of those that were formally presented to the committee were in fact adopted established the equally val-

uable principle that specifically indictable crimes would not
be required for impeachment, thereby helping to assure the
continued healthy survival of a government in which both
the law and the public trust are respected.

☐ The drawn-out, often ponderous nature of impeachment was revealed to be an essential element of the process
itself and an ultimate advantage in securing public trust and
respect for that process. The care and time that went into the
proceedings, while often frustrating, established the process
as one to be used only rarely and only for the most serious
cause.

By consuming the attention of the nation for months, the
process's slowness—dictated by the seriousness of the impeachment remedy and by the way in which that provision
was implemented—established a high burden on those wish-
ing to invoke it: to ensure that the price which the nation
would pay in the loss of attention from other crucial business
of government was justified by the magnitude of the abuse of
trust which led to initiation of the process.

Similarly, the slowness of the process also allowed the
American public to thoroughly examine the evidence laid
out before it and to form judgments based on that evidence
rather than on partisanship. If impeachment had been swift,
it would not have afforded the public any real opportunity to
examine in some detail the charges against the President.
Instead, by drawing the process out over a period of months,
the American people gradually came to know the enormity

182

of the abuses that had been committed and therefore more readily understood the fundamental necessity of seeing the process through to a satisfactory conclusion. By the eve of the resignation of the President, 65 percent of the American people thought that he should be impeached. This was a startling climb from the 19 percent favoring impeachment in June of 1973 and the 38 percent favoring it in February of 1974.

More than anything else, this change showed the convincing evidence that had been placed before the American people. That the Nixon resignation did not create a wave of bitter recrimination testifies to the quality of the evidence and the effectiveness of the impeachment process.

☐ If the impeachment process is to work, we learned that those pursuing that process must have full access to all relevant materials. Here, the Supreme Court decision in the "tapes" case (*U.S. v. Nixon*) is a paradox. The decision requiring full production of subpoenaed evidence was essential to the impeachment proceedings, and the Court's determination that it had the authority to determine the law even against a Presidential assertion to the contrary was an obvious necessity if the judicial branch was to remain coequal. But the longer-range implication of the case on the scope of Presidential powers had some very disturbing implications. For while striking down a Presidential claim to absolute privilege, the opinion declared that the doctrine of Presidential privilege existed, despite the fact that it is not even mentioned in the Constitution. The opinion referred to the "President's need for complete candor," which "calls for great deference from the courts"; acknowledged the "importance of the general privilege of confidentiality of Presidential communications in performance of his responsibilities"; and asserted that this privilege is "fundamental to the operation of government" and is owed a "high degree of deference." The Court cited as possible justification for invoking the Presidential privilege precisely the ground of "diplomatic or sensitive national security secrets" which has sustained the Presidential secrecy system so important to the aggrandizement and unrestrained Presidential powers. And, while the Court's language was *dictum*—unneeded for the decision—I am certain it will be invoked by future Presidents to avoid accountability.

The Court had ordered production of all subpoenaed evidence, but at the same time reaffirmed its reluctance to tangle with Presidents on all but the most unavoidable of controversies. As a result, the Court asserted its jurisdiction as the ultimate arbitrator of disputes involving the boundaries of executive and legislative power, while at the same time giving the nation a warning that the Congress would be required to bear the major burden of restraining illegal Presidential power.

☐ We discovered that impeachment need not tear the nation apart if a majority of the people believe that the grounds for impeachment are solid and that the proceedings leading to impeachment have been fairly and impartially conducted. The strong divisions of opinion on the guilt or innocence of Richard Nixon never became an unhealthy symptom of impending national strife precisely because these divisions were balanced by the public's perception that the proceedings were being undertaken with responsibility and fairness.

The breadth of the pro-impeachment votes on the House Judiciary Committee confirmed this essential fairness for the American public. They appreciated the gravity of the impeachment proceedings, and expected the highest standards of public conduct. Most of the members of the Judiciary Committee who appeared to be acting more out of partisan concerns than an appreciation of the evidence were defeated in the 1974 elections. Americans once again showed their ability to judge character and integrity under the most difficult of circumstances.

☐ We also learned that many other institutions and individuals in our democracy, both inside and outside of government, must do their jobs if Presidential abuses of power are to be brought to justice. Without the courts, the Congress could not have done its job effectively; without the media, neither the courts nor the Congress could have performed their tasks as well as they did. And the functioning of our key institutions was matched by the extraordinary jobs done by men like John Sirica, Sam Ervin, Peter Rodino, Archibald Cox, Elliot Richardson and William Ruckelshaus. They once again reminded us of the necessary blend of strong institutions and strong individuals needed to keep a democracy vital.

None of the institutions involved, however, should be thoroughly satisfied with its performance in handling the impeachment inquiry and the events that led up to it. If Richard Nixon felt that he was above the law and could get away with the illegality he undertook, it was at least in part because our institutions were not doing their jobs as effectively as necessary. And the need for future impeachment proceedings will rest on the ability of Congress, the parties, the media, the courts and the Cabinet to affect Presidential conduct so as to reduce the likelihood of future massive violations of the public trust.

☐ The impeachment proceedings did serve as an excellent reminder that in restraining arbitrary Presidential conduct, other institutions will receive public support if the people perceive these institutions to be functioning effectively and fairly. The sharp rise in the percentage of Americans who believed that Congress was doing a good job—an increase from 30 percent before the televised Judiciary Committee proceedings to 48 percent after—is the most fitting possible rebuttal to the contention that the American public has become so cynical and hardened that it no longer trusts any aspect of government. The Congress can earn the respect of the public only if we deserve that respect, and the lessons of the Nixon impeachment inquiry should continually remind

186

us of the perceptiveness and essential good judgment of the American people.

If much good came from the impeachment inquiry, one enormous act of poor judgment also marred its conclusion. The precipitous and blanket pardon of former President Nixon by President Ford violated two of the most essential elements of the entire process—the need for full disclosure of all relevant information regarding Presidential abuse of power, and the encouragement of a sense of equality of justice. By eliminating the ability to obtain a confession of guilt or a trial of the former President, the pardon destroyed, perhaps forever, the ability of the American people to learn the full story of Watergate. And by violating Theodore Roosevelt's belief that "no man is above the Law," the pardon condoned a dual standard of punishment at odds with the American tradition of equal justice under the law.

The pardon power might have been and still could become the "Catch-22" of the entire impeachment process, particularly in light of the Twenty-fifth Amendment, which permits a President not elected by the people to grant a pardon. The lure of the pardon was clearly used by President Nixon in his offers of executive clemency to buy the silence of Watergate conspirators. Had they been more successful, much of the truth about Watergate might never have become known. Had they been more successful in using the pardon power as a shield against incrimination, the Nixon administration might have forever eliminated the effectiveness of the impeachment weapon, thereby endangering the viability of our democracy.

To help prevent misuse of the pardon power in the future we should enact a constitutional amendment vesting in Congress the ability to override Presidential pardons by a two-thirds vote of both Houses. This override should be used very sparingly; but it should be available to help eliminate the temptation to short-circuit the judicial system.

☐ Yet even the pardon itself—and particularly the very strong public reaction to it—helped affirm what is undoubtedly the most important positive outcome of the entire impeachment struggle: the undeniable fact that the American people still care very much about the way their government is run and will still insist on a government of laws and not of men. The reaction after the "Saturday night massacre," the reaction after the release of edited Nixon tapes, and the reaction after the Presidential pardon of Richard Nixon all reveal this passionate concern of the people for their government and its fairness.

On March 13, 1973, Richard Nixon told John Dean that he felt Watergate would remain manageable because concern with it could be confined to the "upper intellectual types, the soft heads" and the like. Nixon guessed that "average people won't think it is much of a crisis unless it affects them." What Richard Nixon—and Gerald Ford after him—failed to realize is that the American people knew that the massive abuse of the public trust did affect them; they knew that the subversion of the IRS, the CIA, the FBI and the Justice Department *did* affect them; and they knew that the undermining of the integrity of the election and judicial process *did* affect their most vital interests.

Millions of Americans who had supported Richard Nixon throughout his entire political career and who strongly supported his conservative philosophy were honest, concerned and perceptive enough to view the evidence and decide in favor of a procedure which protected the Constitutional framework of our country. And this demonstration of concern and intelligence and willingness to put partisanship aside to save our system should itself be a sobering realization for any future President who might contemplate undertaking another Watergate.

While we can take great satisfaction with much that emerged from the impeachment inquiry, we cannot become self-satisfied. Our system worked, but it worked only with the aid of a good deal of luck and a great deal of hard work. The initial detection of the Watergate burglary, the random selection of Judge John Sirica to preside over a seemingly unimportant burglary case, the accidental assignment of that case to two very junior reporters at the *Washington Post*, the presence of Sam Ervin in the Senate, the throwaway question asked of Alexander Butterfield revealing the existence of the White House tapes—all perhaps stand as a reflection on the peculiar American good fortune that when the danger to our system was most acute, a Frank Wills or a John Sirica was there. But good fortune alone will not preserve a democracy in which there is no will to guard against the abuse of power.

The revelations of illegal and improper conduct which culminated in impeachment proceedings have shown the need for permanent vigilance over the conduct of the executive branch. The firing of Special Watergate Prosecutor Archibald Cox in October of 1973 was the final blow in a series of blows to the public perception that a fair and independent inquiry of the Watergate matter could be made within the executive branch. Richard Nixon's refusal to accept an order of the U.S. Circuit Court of Appeals to surrender Watergate-related tapes for inspection by Judge John Sirica plunged the nation into turmoil. And his decision to attempt to impose a "compromise" on Special Prosecutor Cox—and Cox's refusal to accede to that "compromise"—was a major turning point in the events leading to his recommended impeachment by the House Judiciary Committee.

Broader issues were raised by the Cox firing, however. The Watergate affair made clear to the entire American public that on the most sensitive matters involving potential wrongdoing in the executive branch, obedience to the law was totally in the hands of the President. Because of his control over the Justice Department and therefore the Attorney General, the President controls the very weapons which should be available to others—the Congress as well as the public—to determine whether executive branch officials are performing their tasks responsibly and legally. As the U.S. Supreme Court stated in 1934, in discussing the removal power, "It is quite evident that one who holds his office only during the pleasure of another, cannot be depended upon to maintain an attitude of independence against the latter's will." This is precisely the position in which Justice Department employees were constantly placed. Subject to dismissal by the President, the Attorney General and his subordinates are in reality not free agents when dealing with executive branch wrongdoing. They are rather agents of the President, and cannot always be depended upon to exercise the independence needed to protect the integrity of governmental processes in the face of wrongdoing.

The dilemma of the Justice Department employee was clearly shown by Henry Petersen's behavior during the Watergate investigation and cover-up. Petersen was head of the department's Criminal Division and a career civil servant with a distinguished record in the department. Yet the Watergate tapes show that he served as a conduit for information from the grand jury and the Watergate prosecutors through John Dean and ultimately to Richard Nixon. As John Dean boasted to the President, Petersen was "the only man I know ... that really could tell us how this could be put together so that it did the maximum to carve it away with a minimum damage to individuals involved."

At one point, Petersen told the President that the Watergate investigation would not reach him because the Department of Justice simply did not have the power to investigate the President. "We have no mandate to investigate the President," Petersen said. "We investigate Watergate. . . . My understanding of law is—my understanding of our responsibilities is—that if it came to that I would have to come to [U.S. Attorney Harold] Titus and say, 'We can't do that.' The only people who have jurisdiction to do that is the House of Representatives, as far as I'm concerned." In fact, of course, his oath of office should have led him to seek enforcement of *all* laws.

Clearly, control of the prosecution function was a major part of the Nixon containment strategy. Just as clearly, there was very little that Congress or the courts could do as long as the dependence of the prosecutor on the Chief Executive remained. Because of this obvious problem, the Congress considered in the winter of 1973 legislation to establish an office of special prosecutor independent from the President. Under provisions of this legislation, the U.S. District Court for the District of Columbia would be vested with power to remove the special prosecutor for gross impropriety, dereliction of duty or incapacity. In addition, the Congress could impeach him or simply abolish the office of special prosecutor. But outside of these limitations, he would have been free from interference or control by either the judiciary or executive branches.

While this legislation was aimed at establishment of a special prosecutor with a mandate to investigate Watergate-related matters, I believe there is a need for an office of public attorney to undertake investigations on a broader range of issues, free from executive branch interference. The duties of this permanent office of public attorney would include prosecuting in cases of allegation of conflict of interest within the executive, inquiring into alleged misconduct within the executive branch, and prosecuting cases of election law violations referred to the office by the Federal Elections Commission established in the Federal Election Campaign Act of 1974. The public attorney would be judicially appointed, subject to Senate confirmation, and would serve a limited term in that office.

Some have questioned the constitutionality of establishing a prosecutor outside the executive branch. I believe, however, that the fact that a public attorney would be judicially appointed does not destroy the separation of powers any more than the Presidential appointment of judges means that a President is performing a judicial function. In fact, establishment of this type of independent office would aid, rather than destroy, the separation of powers. As the report of the Senate Judiciary Committee noted in recommending establishment of a special Watergate prosecutor:

> Under the Constitution, power is dispersed among the three separate branches of government so that each might check and balance the others—not to insulate the President from effective control. To invoke the separa-

tion of powers doctrine to prevent independent investigations of criminal conduct in the executive branch is to stand the doctrine on its head.

Establishing an office of public attorney, with full power to gain access to executive branch records and the full range of criminal investigatory powers, would both help prevent illegal activity from occurring and would help bring to justice any who might undertake such activity. And I believe that knowledge by the American people that there was a permanent watchdog on executive branch activity—not subject to removal by the President or any other executive branch official—would do much to reestablish confidence in the ability of government to really investigate itself and ensure that respect of the law is maintained. Hopefully, it would be one more step we could take to help reduce the likelihood of and need for another Presidential impeachment proceeding.

No institutional reform can ever eliminate the possibility of another President, perhaps in different ways, with different motives and with different personnel, attempting to rob us of our freedoms. No reform can ensure us against another President committing offenses so grave that the impeachment process may once again be needed. And certainly no reform can ever guarantee the good fortune which seems to guard our system at moments of peril.

But institutional changes, along with the renewed vitality of the impeachment process itself, can create a psychology of Presidential restraint and the recognition of the high political price exacted for lack of restraint which will make gross illegality and impropriety less likely to darken our national scene again. The creation of this psychology in our Presidents—and indeed throughout the executive branch—will require constant vigilance.

But the goal of assuring Presidential respect for the law as the basis of our democracy is well worth that effort.

At some time in the future, impeachment may once again—despite our efforts—be called on to fulfill its constitutional function. Should this occur, we would once again be forced to reflect on how our constitutional system and the individuals who control that system had been found wanting. And once again we would hopefully be able to marvel at the wisdom of the framers in substituting, through the impeachment process, what Alexander Hamilton termed the "mild magistracy of the law for the terrible weapon of the sword."

8

The Fourth Estate

The President
and the Media

If the government and the officers of it are to be the constant theme for newspaper abuse, and this too without condescending to investigate the motives or the facts, it will be impossible, I conceive, for any man living to manage the helm or to keep the machine together.

—George Washington

The hand that rules the press, the radio, the screen, and the far-spread magazine rules the country; whether we like it or not, we must learn to accept it.

—Learned Hand

Throughout our history, the relationship between Presidents and the news media has been turbulent and often emotional. Presidents have sparred with the media; they have threatened and attempted to intimidate them; they have flattered and attempted to woo them. No matter what the approach, however, the interaction between President and media has been a continual source of tension.

196

The reason is clear: The media have probed government and reported the facts and the views of dissenting groups within our society. They have informed the public and created the dialogue without which democracy cannot survive. Walter Lippmann once remarked that the press "dares to be independent of the political power."

Clearly, he realized that the media must be free to inform the American people, and they dare not be coopted by government. The media have been and must continue to be the messengers bringing the bad news—as well as the good —to the American people and to the President. And the tension that results from this adversary relationship between President and media is absolutely crucial.

Yet in recent years, this relationship has been threatened. Presidents have all too often been given a way out of the dilemma of how to deal with a feisty media corps. Presidents have tried to immunize themselves from the struggle with the media through their government's control over the very media which should be probing and criticizing Presidential actions.

The immense power of radio and television has brought about this historically significant shift toward Presidential power and influence. Theodore Roosevelt said that Presidents occupied the "bully pulpit" in gaining public attention. Today, announcements from that bully pulpit are heard and seen instantaneously and nationally by millions of Americans because of Presidential domination of radio and television, usually without the right of equal media coverage of congressional, political party or other dissenting views. The decline of Presidential accountability is in part the result of this incredible advantage arising from Presidential domination of the nation's electronic media.

Over history, our Presidents have been remarkable for their consistency in denouncing the media as unfair, uninformed and unmanageable because they have continually pointed out the facts and realities which any administration would often prefer to evade or ignore. George Washington's laments about the "newspaper abuse" which he was suffering were repeated by most of our Presidents. Jefferson thought that even the least informed "have learnt that nothing in a newspaper is to be believed," and Wilson, over one hundred years later, echoed them in complaining that he was so used to having "everything reported erroneously that I have almost come to the point of believing nothing that I see in the newspapers." Teddy Roosevelt, who enjoyed dealing with the press, could nevertheless have his Attorney General sue two newspapers for criminal libel, a suit which he later lost. John Kennedy, a master at press relations, could nevertheless protest just before the Bay of Pigs invasion that "Castro doesn't need agents over there. All he has to do is read our papers. It's all laid out for him." Lyndon Johnson's irritability with the news media was matched only by his voracious appetite for learning of their latest barbs, and Richard Nixon's fear of the media was equaled only by his continuing attempts to control them.

The themes are common ones, which transcend ideology and political party: Presidents dislike the news media because the media investigate the truth behind executive actions, place facts in their historical setting, and provide Americans with the information needed to judge Presidential performance. In a way, Presidents throughout our history have seemed to think—or, at least, hope—that the media belonged to them, and have often seemed resentful when that has not been the case.

Whatever the cause, the strong reactions which Presidents have often expressed when confronted by media criticism, or exposure of wrongdoing in their administration, or other unwanted disclosures have often led to Presidential attempts to blunt the media's impact. Over one hundred years ago, Andrew Jackson thought he had found one means of dealing with balky newspapers by adding fifty-seven journalists to the government payroll. John Kennedy's social flattery of the Washington press corps is well known and prompted Arthur Krock to charge that "a news management policy not only exists, but in the form of direct and deliberate actions has been enforced more cynically and boldly than by any other previous administration." And when Richard Nixon failed in his effort to coopt the media, he tried to destroy their independence. Vice-President Agnew was sent forth to deliberately discredit and harass the media, aided by the President himself and the chairman of the Republican National Committee; subpoenas directed at the media emerged from the Justice Department; the very existence and independence of public television was threatened by an administration campaign of harassment; and for the first time in the nation's history, an administration succeeded in temporarily censoring a newspaper—the *New York Times*—from printing valuable documentation on the history and origins of our involvement in Vietnam, the so-called Pentagon Papers.

By the end of the first Nixon term, this cynical policy had begun to pay off. David Wise, in an interview with Tom Wicker of the *New York Times,* quoted Wicker as telling of a phone call he had received from James Reston in the summer of 1971. "Scotty called me from Washington. I was in New York and something had come up about the Sheehan [Pentagon Papers] case. I said, 'I don't think we ought to talk about this on the phone.' I don't know if they were listening, but if they can make us feel that way, hell, they've won the game already." Fortunately, the game was not lost for the media; indeed, the diligence of the media in the face of enormous pressure was subsequently in good part responsible for the end of the Nixon squeeze play on both the media and the civil liberties of Americans.

Vietnam and Watergate had shown the ferocity of Presidential reaction to the investigative reporting which is one vital component of free media. And, in the process, those reactions had once again reaffirmed the media's crucial role in serving as a restraint on the consciences and, hopefully, the actions of future Presidents.

In spite of the media's success in helping reveal the

weaknesses and even cynicism behind our Vietnam involvement and the massive assault on our liberties known as Watergate, there is much cause for concern that the cumulative weight of recent expansions of Presidential power will continue to put pressure on the media. The problem of intimidation of the printed media is serious. But the problems of intimidation and manipulation of the electronic media are even more dangerous because of control of those media by the federal government. And, unless changes are instituted, Presidents will continue to try to dominate the electronic communications media.

For while Presidents have consistently criticized and pressured the media, they have also been most adept at using them for their own benefit. Basic to the effective Presidential use of the media have been three tools: the President's use of radio and television as a nationwide forum for the presentation of his viewpoint, the Presidential news conference, and the White House and executive branch public relations machine. Each of these tools has been adapted to suit the needs and preferences of individual Presidents; all have helped to amplify the Presidential voice and muffle dissenting voices calling for restraint on Presidential actions.

Surely the most important and dangerous change in Presidential power over the media has been the domination by Presidents of the electronic media. The real revolution in communication by government has been a television revolution, whose potential Presidents have exploited with regularity and with skill. Today, 97 percent of American households have at least one television set, and television has almost certainly become the nation's single most important source of news. A recent Louis Harris survey found that 65 percent of those polled indicated television as an important news source, surpassing the 52 percent rating given newspapers. This dramatic change in Americans' sources of information and news has had a massive effect on the ways in which government communicates with the people and in the ability of people to accurately perceive the nature of their government.

Most importantly, in television recent Presidents have found a new and very powerful instrument, which they seem to regard as their own with every bit as much ferocity as the most possessive child views his most cherished toy. Perhaps only this can explain the intensity of Presidential displeasure when the television networks "misbehave," and the attempts of recent administrations to use the vulnerability of the electronic media to attempt to enforce conformity. Though newspapers have been the consistent target of pressures from Presidents, the greater power of television is accompanied by a greater vulnerability to that Presidential pressure, because of the licensing requirements with which the nation's press need not concern itself. The Federal Communications Commission has tremendous power, through its power to license network station outlets and its ability to control the terms under which political debate and discussion are aired. And because the President nominates members of the FCC, his indirect power over the commission is substantial, though Congress does retain the power of confirming the commissioners.

Presidents Kennedy and Johnson used subtle and sometimes not-so-subtle pressures on those television networks which had incurred their wrath. For Kennedy, there was an occasional outburst to a top aide or even to the FCC chairman that the networks had gone too far and that something had to be done about it. With Johnson, the outbursts and threats were intermixed with invitations of key television journalists for pleasant weekends on the Perdanales. Neither method was particularly appealing, but neither President sought in an organized way to cripple the media. That bold attempt was made by Richard Nixon.

While the Nixon campaign to undermine the credibility of the press was intense, his strategy to destroy the independence of radio and television threatened the vitality of American democracy. While Spiro Agnew villified the *Washington Post* and the *New York Times*, the impact of Nixon administration criticisms of the networks was undoubtedly greater. Dean Burch, former Republican Party chairman, who was appointed Federal Communications Commission chairman shortly before the first of Agnew's major attacks on the media, called heads of the networks in November of 1969 and demanded copies of their commentaries on a recent Presidential speech on Vietnam. As David Wise comments, "To the networks, the signals were plain enough; by his words and actions, the theoretically independent chairman of the FCC was supporting the Vice-President." And by the end of 1972, with Watergate beginning to drag down his administration, Richard Nixon's hatred of the *Washington Post* for its Watergate coverage found an outlet with a Presidential outburst regarding the *Post*'s television stations. "The main thing is the *Post* is going to have damnable, damnable problems out of this one. They have a television station . . . and they're going to have to get it renewed." The greater vulnerability of the electronic media because of their need for government licenses was going to be exploited to the fullest.

The Nixon administration also attempted to subvert the spirit and intent of the Public Broadcasting Act of 1967. When passed, this Act aimed at development of a significant alternative to the major commercial television networks, a voice free to express views and opinions not ordinarily available through private television. Yet as part of the administration's campaign against the media, pressure was brought to bear against the Corporation for Public Broadcasting in an attempt to reshape the image of public television in the administration's liking. In November of 1971, John Witherspoon, director of television activities for the Corporation for Public Broadcasting, put it bluntly. Witherspoon said that a speech given by Clay Whitehead, chief of White House

Office of Telecommunications Policy, had made clear "in straightforward political language that until public broadcasting shows signs of becoming what this administration wants it to be, this administration will oppose permanent financing."

And that prediction proved to be accurate. In June of 1972, President Nixon vetoed legislation authorizing two years of funding for public television at a total funding level of $155 million. And, unfortunately, the Congress bowed to the President and passed legislation calling only for a one-year authorization of public television at a level of $45 million.

The Nixon administration also attempted to remove much of the controversial opinion from public television by attempting to end programs such as "Bill Moyer's Journal," Elizabeth Drew's "Thirty Minutes With," "Washington Week in Review," and William Buckley's "Firing Line." Though many of these programs were subsequently saved, the intent was clear: to enforce an ideological blandness and uniformity on public television which reflected the Nixon administration's point of view. Another potential voice of dissent would be silenced.

All this, however, seemed to be mere rehearsal for the attack on the independence of the electronic media, which quite clearly was planned for the second term of the Nixon administration, had not the media's uncovering of Watergate put the administration on the defensive. Clay Whitehead signaled the beginning of open season on the networks when, shortly after the landslide victory of November 1972, he warned the networks that their license renewals might now become dependent on the ideology of their news operations. "Station managers and network officials who fail to act to correct imbalance or consistent bias in the networks, or who acquiesce by silence, can only be considered willing participants to be held fully accountable at license renewal time." Since imbalance, like beauty, is in the eye of the beholder, Whitehead's threat was not lost on the networks. His warning of retaliation against networks and stations reporting what he called "ideological plugola" was taken by them as an open threat against their reporting materials critical to the Nixon Presidency.

This type of abuse of Presidential power cannot be allowed to occur ever again if the potential of radio and television is to become an influence for diversity, rather than conformity, in our society. We must ensure that both private and public electronic media are kept free of Presidential pressure and capable of serving the national interest and not the interests of the White House.

For the private sector, I believe this may require the granting of license periods by the Federal Communications Commission for longer than the present three-year period. Extending the period of license renewal for television outlets would help reduce the temptation for Presidents to resort to threats as a means of enforcing ideological uniformity. In view of the undoubted domination of radio and television as the source for public information and comment, threats by the government directed toward networks and their outlets must be viewed as a fundamental risk to full and free news coverage. I am so convinced of the seriousness of this risk that I have changed my mind and now believe that licenses granted by the FCC should be for periods which in most cases exceed the term of an incumbent administration. The present three years is simply not enough, and should be extended to at least five years, and perhaps longer. Only with such protection can the owners of radio and television outlets resist Presidential and FCC pressure to intimidate them from giving unbiased news coverage. Some have argued that longer license renewal periods would diminish the ability of television outlets to serve their local communities. But I believe that concern is best met by insisting that there be competition in media outlets through independent, competing ownership at the local level.

In addition, we must invigorate the public television network in this country into becoming what it was originally designed to be: a voice independent of government and the private communications media. The struggles which have taken place in recent years over public television must be put behind us. Through a combination of increased long-term funding, a truly independent board of directors and a commitment from any administration in power to keep attempts at political control out of public television we must attempt to provide a media alternative which will truly increase the variety of viewpoints offered the American public.

Insulating radio and television from political intimidation to assure their independence is part of the answer. But it is not enough, because even without Presidential intimidation, the present system of laws and regulations allows Presidents to dominate the use of the electronic media. And they have clearly recognized the importance of these media for their own purposes. The frequency of their appearances proves the point. John Kennedy's ten television reports to the nation, while revolutionizing the Presidential use of the medium, must be compared with Lyndon Johnson's twenty-four and Richard Nixon's seventy-nine.

As Newton Minow and his co-authors have illustrated in *Presidential Television,* Nixon made as many prime-time appearances during his first eighteen months in office as the combined appearances of Eisenhower, Kennedy and Johnson during their first similar periods in office.

The reasons for the growing popularity of "Presidential television" are clear and simple: it is an effective tool for shaping public opinion, particularly when Presidents only rarely need face any opposing viewpoint in response. Survey data have indicated consistent increases in public support for Presidential actions after Presidential appearances on television, including a dramatic jump from 7 percent approval to

50 percent approval of President Nixon's Cambodian invasion in April of 1970. The ineffectiveness—indeed the negative effect—on his personal popularity of most of President Nixon's televised appearances explaining Watergate does show that, as with the televised news conference, the special Presidential address is not without its dangers. But on the vast majority of issues, the use of television for special appearances by Presidents affords all the advantages of television exposure with none of the disadvantages of the pesky questions.

The President sits in isolated splendor, with the umbilical cord of television connecting him directly with a hundred million American homes. And, perhaps most enviable of all from the Presidential perspective, the opposition party and the Congress have no effective means of replying. The fairness doctrine, the equal time provisions, the political party doctrines—all, as we have seen, are ineffective in the context of a politcal campaign in giving the opposition candidate the ability to compete. And their power is no less impressive in preserving the near monopoly of Presidential use of television in a non-campaign context, if indeed such a context ever truly exists.

The Nixon years offer ample proof of this near monopoly. In his five and a half years in office, Richard Nixon made a total of seventy-nine appearances on television, forty-three of them in prime time. The Democratic opposition could obtain only twelve appearances, with just five in prime time and only two of those broadcast simultaneously on all three networks. Thus even the limited number of congressional and party responses usually appeared at less desirable times, without benefit of simultaneous broadcast on all three networks, and with lower viewership. In the light of these favorable odds for Presidents, it was not surprising that President Nixon attempted to ridicule and eliminate the so-called instant analysis of Presidential addresses by professional newsmen immediately following those addresses. This remains one of the few available opportunities for other voices to be heard, before the same audience, capable of raising the tough questions to be considered by the public in evaluating Presidential statements. And because congressional and opposing party responses are so limited, so-called instant analysis is important and must be continued.

Television networks probably resist equal time requests from the Congress or the parties because they interrupt regular programming. But they obviously find it much easier to resist congressional pressure than to resist Presidential pressure. The networks fear FCC pressure if they resist the "requests" of any President for air time, since the FCC tends to be dominated by nominees of an incumbent administration and the pressure which it can exert is substantial.

In October of 1974, less than one month before congressional elections took place, President Ford traveled to Kansas City to deliver a speech on inflation to the Future Farmers of America. The White House—worried about the President's standing with the public—wanted the speech carried on television, even though it subsequently was clear that there was little new in the speech. The networks resisted, and the White House responded with a formal request for broadcast time. The result was immediate compliance by all three networks. As William Sheehan, president of ABC News, commented, "Historically, any time a President flat-out asks for air time, he'll get it. . . . When the President wants to speak to the nation there's no way we can deny him the air."

Whatever Presidents want, Presidents get. And they seem to want television time so badly that I suspect if they were offered one or the other—giving up their veto power or forgoing their unlimited access to radio and television—they would probably forgo the veto power.

The use of unanswered radio and television by our recent Presidents therefore has presented us with two important problems which must be overcome if the power of television is to benefit our political process. First, Presidents—at least since Lyndon Johnson—have been the sole determinants of when, how and for how long they will use television. And second, there have been no other voices which have possessed that power and which were able to compete with Presidents for a public audience. As a result, another powerful barrier has been erected in the path of establishing restraints that force our Chief Executive to realize that his views will be answered by other dissenting voices that will be given equal prominence with his own.

Congress has failed to vigorously exercise its rights and the rights of the political parties to the electronic media. The laws establishing the basic regulatory power over the airwaves have been fashioned by the Congress; the commissioners of the FCC have been confirmed by Congress; and yet little has been done institutionally to prepare an effective response to the use of television by Presidents as a medium for personalizing leadership and reducing the effectiveness of the Congress and the parties.

Until very recently, Congress has simply failed to recognize the potential influence of television on both its own institutional effectiveness and that of the parties. As John Stewart pointed out in a report prepared for the Joint Committee on Government Operations:

> Contrasting with the awareness demonstrated by Presidents of the critical role that mass communications would play in the governing process, Congress has followed a much more passive course. Innovation by Congress in mass communications at the institutional level is rare and hard to find. . . . In 1947, television cameras were permitted in the House Chamber to cover the opening session of the 80th Congress. . . . This coverage of the 80th Congress was a television first— and last—since film and electronic cameras have never again been permitted in either chamber to cover a regular congressional session. There is irony, to say the least, in the fact that Congress does permit coverage of

presidential addresses to joint sessions of the Congress in the House chamber, as well as speeches by other non-congressional dignitaries, such as astronauts and visiting heads of state.

The missed opportunities which this failure to use the power of television has caused were effectively demonstrated by the upsurge in public opinion indicators of support for the Congress in the wake of the televised House Judiciary Committee impeachment inquiry proceedings. Those proceedings were obviously not typical of the more routine aspects of congressional business and were still not a full use of television to cover debates of the entire House. Nevertheless, the interest those hearings received should encourage the Congress to move more quickly in recognizing the potential of the television revolution and responding creatively to it.

There are dangers, to be sure. The last thing the American people need is a congressional replication of Presidential and executive branch public relations techniques. If the use of television by Congress must imply such a result, more harm than good would likely to be achieved by its adoption. But the very diversity of Congress, which has been one barrier preventing effective and adequate television exposure, is also a safeguard against a monolithic, congressional public relations point of view of the type in which the executive branch so often indulges.

There is no single institutional change which is enough; rather a need exists for a variety of ideas to encourage exposure of congressional, party and media viewpoints. We need a continuation of "instant analysis" of Presidential addresses by seasoned newsmen and newswomen. We should require by law that the major television networks give equal time for reply by congressional opposition party leaders to any Presidential address, even if not in a Presidential campaign period. And this right of reply should be given on the same terms as the Presidential address. If the President appeared on all three networks in prime time, the opposition should be accorded a similar right—within forty-eight hours of the time of the Presidential address. There is little point in giving a right of reply to a Presidential address if the President speaks on all three networks at 8:00 P.M. and the opposition reply comes at separate and less useful hours.

There will be problems, of course, in determining who will be given a right to reply and who in fact really represents the opposition in a non-parliamentary system such as ours. But these problems can be solved.

Similarly, the reforms suggested earlier must be implemented to further assure access to debate and discussion between candidates during a Presidential campaign. Particularly if a campaign involves an incumbent President, the need for continuous, searching debate in a wide variety of formats throughout the campaign is vital in reducing the ability of Presidents to gain re-election without a complete

214

examination of their views and character by the media and the people.

Another step of great importance in redressing the present Presidential-congressional imbalance would be a thorough opening up of congressional proceedings to coverage by the electronic media. Congress is beginning to move in this direction through opening up to the public—and therefore to media coverage—most committee executive sessions and conference committees between House and Senate, and through a growing movement to allow electronic media coverage of full House and Senate sessions. I believe all these sessions must be made available to full radio and television coverage unless specific and convincing reasons can be advanced for closing a particular session.

Although a variety of scheduled formats are possible in opening up Congress to radio and television, I believe those decisions should be left to the networks themselves. Congress should not get into the business of "staging" productions for the American viewing and listening public. The coverage given the Army-McCarthy hearings, the Senate Foreign Relations Committee hearings on Vietnam, the Watergate Committee and the House Judiciary Committee impeachment inquiry prove that radio and television will cover meaningful congressional proceedings, and that the American people will listen and learn from them. We should simply open up our sessions and go about our jobs with the knowledge that all our proceedings can be covered by the media. They can then decide what deserves coverage on the basis of the news value of our actions. Indeed, this would be a strong incentive for the Congress to streamline its procedures, make its debates more relevant, and present itself as a body at work on the serious problems facing the nation and the world.

As discussed earlier, institution of a regularly televised question-and-report period, during which Cabinet officers would answer questions from the entire Senate, would enable the public to see both the Congress and the executive debating crucial issues. Numerous question periods on Vietnam or Watergate could have been of real value. And future question periods on such issues as energy, inflation, unemployment, education and health care could be useful educational tools for the American people.

The amount of coverage the networks give the Congress should depend on the type of job we are doing. Our ability to stick to the principal issues facing the nation would gain us the media coverage needed to put the Congress on a more equal media footing with the President. Our job is to use the House and Senate floors, the committees of both Houses, and, in particular, the select committees established to investigate particular problems as national forums to get across a perspective that competes with that of the President. And when we do that job effectively, one massive Presidential power not anticipated by the Constitution—the domination by our Presidents of the mass media—will be greatly weakened.

The political parties must also be given greater exposure to the American public through the electronic media if they are to become more effective. And this exposure cannot only come during the months immediately preceding a Presidential election. Rather, it must be more constant, with representatives of the major parties discussing and debating national issues. As in the case of the Congress, I do not believe the parties should attempt to "stage" events expressly designed for radio and television. But they should work harder in trying to devise ways to make their proceedings and discussions more interesting and timely, and thereby, hopefully, of more interest to the electronic media.

The Democratic Midterm Convention in Kansas City is one good example of the type of event which received widespread media attention because issues of importance were being discussed. The highly successful Democratic Party telethons, for which party chairman Bob Strauss deserves great credit, are a different and yet effective way of helping the party financially and of making the American people more aware of party leaders and purposes. And the series of debates around the country staged in 1974 between Senators Lloyd Bentsen and Bill Brock, in their roles as chairmen of the Democratic and Republican Senatorial Campaign Committees, also offers promise for attracting more media interest.

If party events are newsworthy, they will more likely be covered; and if they are covered by the media, Americans will come to know their political parties better. Hopefully, these party events will also give the opportunity for introducing to the public not only members of Congress but also the many talented men and women who are governors, mayors or other local officials. All too often, we overlook the great talent available outside Washington; and, hopefully, increased media attention to party events will allow more exposure for these individuals and thereby help widen the pool of potential Presidential candidates.

Just as the Presidential use of television in general has revolutionized relations between Presidents and the people, so has television and radio affected another of the principal Presidential media tools—the Presidential news conference.

The Presidential news conference is a strange and wondrous creature, with a checkered history which makes up in color what it lacks in longevity. Though Grover Cleveland began meeting informally with selected members of the press in 1885, not until the administration of Woodrow Wilson did the news conference begin to take shape. Its evolution has been unsteady and almost totally dependent on the vagaries of Presidential personality; yet the ability of Presidents to use the media to their advantage through the news conference has grown with the age of television and the availability of instant communication reaching tens of millions of Americans.

The format of the news conference has seen many changes over the years. The tradition began with Wilson, then took a giant step backward during the 1920s when written questions were required after President Harding had touched off a worldwide diplomatic incident because of an indiscreet answer to a reporter's question.

Only with Franklin Roosevelt did the questions become spontaneous once again, with heated exchanges. Eisenhower opened the Pandora's box of the televised news conference for later broadcast, and John Kennedy completed the evolution by allowing live coverage of the event. This variety in format had been equaled by a similar variety in frequency. Franklin Roosevelt held 998 of them in his thirteen years as President; Richard Nixon's fear of the media resulted in a grand total of 37 news conferences in over five years in office.

The institution was flexible enough to suit the needs of successive Presidents and the developments of expanding technologies. Yet while those needs continued to vary over time, the demands of those technologies have taken their toll on the value of the news conference as a medium for exchanging ideas and informing Presidents. In fact, radio and television have greatly increased the ability of Presidents to use the news conference as another means of going over the heads of the Congress and the parties directly to the American people. As the late Merriman Smith accurately observed:

> Mr. Roosevelt debated with reporters. He insulted them, lectured them, and made them laugh. He called

them liars, and used the mighty weight of his high office against the press in pulverizing fashion. Mr. Truman tried to keep everybody happy. His conferences were fast, produced a lot of news, and made the reporters wish they had learned shorthand. Truman was the last President to engage in truly head to head exchanges in not only questions and answers, but also ideas, with reporters. Since then, however, the White House Presidential press conference has become more and more a one-way street, an avenue by which the Chief Executive makes careful policy statements and pretty well sticks to them.

There have been some fundamental changes since the days of Roosevelt's news conferences. The days of head-to-head confrontation between reporters asking the truly tough questions and Presidents willing to engage in real debate seem to be over. And those newsmen—such as CBS's Dan Rather—who are willing to ask the unwanted questions run the risk of corporate disfavor by networks and outlets who fear for the licenses of their company-owned stations.

But the news conference does have value for a number of reasons. By allowing the American people to see their President, the news conference can detect flaws in Presidential leadership as effectively as it can promote that leadership. Richard Nixon held only nine news conferences during his second term in office, and yet each of them helped affirm

what the *New York Times* long ago called the principal
function of the institution: "to provide the nation with a
contemporary portrait of its President." Much as the demeanor of a witness affects the jury's perception of his credibility, so the demeanor of Richard Nixon as he continually
revised his version of Watergate "reality" to fit the pressures
of successive revelations affected the American public's
judgment of his truthfulness. Television had taken its toll on
Richard Nixon once again, and the ability of the television
camera to mirror Presidential personality had performed
perhaps its greatest public service.

If used properly by the media, however, the Presidential
news conference can be much more than a Presidential
public relations gimmick or a video lie detector for the
American public. It can perform a legitimate leadership
function, which, if coupled with the provision of similar
access to spokesmen of the Congress and the opposition
party, can increase public dialogues on issues of importance.
But most importantly, the Presidential news conference can
be a learning, as well as teaching, tool for Presidents. Sidney
Hyman in 1963 described the in-depth preparation President Kennedy underwent to get ready for his news conferences, and the value of those preparations:

> It all makes for a nerve-racking experience and, in
> one sense, a frustrating one. Only very few of the im-
> portant questions the President is prepared to answer

are ever asked at the conference itself. But in a larger sense, it is invaluable. The President is compelled by the pressures of the occasion to make certain he is informed about all the significant events that touch upon his Administration.

The news conference, even in its present form, is one of the most tangible remaining Presidential life-lines to the harsh world of political reality. By forcing a President to concentrate on a wide variety of possible questions, it focuses his attention on areas which might otherwise go unnoticed. And by forcing him to face reporters, it requires a President to at least go through the motions of responding to the unpleasant as well as the welcome inquiry.

There are problems in the present format of the news conference which have reduced its effectiveness. The presence of the electronic media has made news conferences more subject to exercises in Presidential showmanship. With two hundred reporters jamming each televised Presidential news conference, the ability to ask probing questions which will not seem "disrespectful" of the President is greatly diminished. And the demands of television often mean that news conferences must be cut short to fit the necessities of a television schedule, rather than allowing all the important questions to be asked.

We need more news conferences and we need more varied news conferences to help overcome these problems. In addition to the present televised news conference, there is a need for less massive and less formal sessions, not necessarily televised or broadcast on radio, at which smaller groups of reporters could carry on more of a dialogue on issues with a President. Here, hopefully, the tough questions could be asked and pursued more thoroughly than in a more formal setting.

Particularly during Presidential campaigns, the media should require an incumbent President running for re-election to face reporters on a regular basis. The price for Presidential incumbents running for re-election who refuse to do so should be severe: not simply an editorial denouncing a President's refusal to answer questions but perhaps some type of reduction in coverage of the prepared materials always handed out in abundance during Presidential campaigns. There is simply no reason why Richard Nixon should have received coverage of most prepared "handouts" issued during the 1972 campaign at the same time he refused to hold news conferences to face reporters' questions surrounding Watergate or the Vietnam War. Although under current law such "retaliation" would be difficult for the regulated broadcast media, the written press should be under no restrictions in their ability to force Presidents to be responsive during a Presidential campaign.

More varied and more frequent news conferences cannot be legislated. They must develop both from Presidential personalities which do not view the press as enemies or tools for public relations exploitation and from reporters who are determined to be relentless in their pursuit of the facts and unwilling to become passive participants in a Presidential public relations exercise. The news conference does have a legitimate role in fostering Presidential leadership. But only if that role is coupled with an equally insistent search for other roles designed to increase Presidential accountability to the media will this valuable institution realize its full potential.

The third tool used in Presidential control of the media is less dramatic but nevertheless important.

The public relations machinery of the executive branch has grown from an informal collection of small bureaus to a monster of enormous proportions. Every attempt to obtain an accurate accounting of just how many people are engaged in publicity and public relations functions has been basically unsuccessful. We do know that a 1971 survey conducted by the Office of Management and Budget revealed that over six thousand people in the executive branch were engaged in public relations activity at an estimated annual cost of about $164 million. This estimate, which excluded the PR staff of the White House itself, is undoubtedly grossly understated, in part because an obscure law passed in 1913 makes any payments to "publicity experts" illegal without congressional approval. As a result, the executive branch departments and agencies have shown no lack of inventiveness in creating titles for personnel engaged in publicity activities which do not run afoul of the law and which make any meaningful accounting of their true numbers exceedingly difficult. Even the OMB survey, however, raises substantial questions regarding the need for such massive publicity operations by the departments and agencies. Does the Pentagon really need to be "sold" by public relations activities which OMB calculates at over $48 million per year? Does NASA need to spend nearly $15 million to advertise its wares, or HEW over $32 million to make its mission known?

Certainly, there is a legitimate need for familiarizing the public with many of the activities and programs of the executive branch departments. But the line between informational activity and government propaganda is a very thin one indeed. And while much of the everyday executive branch publicity is in no meaningful way controlled by our Presidents, the presence of a massive and well-oiled public relations machine enables Presidents—when the special occasions warrant—to get across their message in a manner unparalleled in our society.

In addition to the large departmental PR apparatus, the White House also has a publicity establishment of its own. Under the Nixon administration there were over sixty people in the White House working on public relations at a total cost to the American taxpayer of hundreds of thousands of dollars per year. And while the Nixon public relations apparatus was larger in size than that of any previous administration, it did not suddenly spring forth from nowhere. Presidents have attempted both to coerce and coopt the media since the beginning of the republic, and the use of hired White House employees in this effort has a long history.

One important means of obtaining information from the executive branch and counteracting some of the propaganda pressure which executive branch publicity generates is through the Freedom of Information Act. The Act, adopted in 1966, was intended to enable the media and the public to secure documents from government agencies which will provide them with the information they need. Unfortunately, because of procedural provisions in the original 1966 Act, the federal bureaucracies had all too often been successful in thwarting the intent of the Act.

Every day, there were "cover-ups" undertaken by federal agencies which helped undermine the confidence of the American people in their government and made it more difficult for the media to do their job well. Even so, valuable information was obtained regarding FBI counterintelligence operations, abuse of the IRS by the Nixon White House through indiscriminate investigations of organizations in the black community, as well as a variety of consumer and health-oriented information.

In 1974, the Congress voted overwhelmingly to amend the Freedom of Information Act to make it easier for its provisions to truly work by reducing the ability of federal agencies to delay and harass those seeking information. Despite his commitment to openness in government, President Ford vetoed this legislation, but fortunately his veto was overridden and these changes were enacted into law.

There are no magic solutions to the problem of governmental propagandizing. The public has a legitimate need for information on the activities of its government. But the Congress should review all department and agency appropriations to see whether they have gone beyond this legitimate public information function, as has been alleged regarding the Defense Department. And we must couple our ability to obtain the information that the executive branch wants us to know with a vigorous use of the Freedom of Information Act to find out what the executive does not want us to know, but which we must find out to get at the truth.

The friction that has existed for almost two hundred years between Presidents and the media has helped to keep our democracy alive and functioning. That friction must be preserved and adapted to modern conditions if the Presidential perspective is not to become further removed from the accountability which the media helps foster.

Healthy and flourishing media can help restrain arbitrary Presidential conduct. They can bring scandal to light, reveal deception, and provide fuller background and information to permit a better public judgment on vital issues. But the media need other institutions—notably the Congress and the political parties—to help in this process of fully informing the public and permitting them to participate more meaningfully in the great public debates we need. To more fully achieve this, the Congress and the parties must retain their capacity to respond to Presidential initiatives. And to do so, they must insist on fairer and fuller access to the electronic media and protections which further the independence of radio and television in the reporting of uncensored news and comment.

9

In Need of Revival

The President and the Parties

The bounty of the American economy, the fluidity of American society, the remarkable unity of the American people, and most important, the success of the American experiment, have all mitigated against the emergence of large dissenting groups that would seek satisfaction of their special needs through the formation of [new] political parties.

—Clinton Rossiter, 1962

For much of American history the party has been the ultimate vehicle for political expression. Voters inherited their politics as they did their religion. It was as painful to desert one's party as one's church. But this has begun to change. . . . By the 1970s ticket-splitting had become common. Independent voting was spreading everywhere, especially among the young. Never had party loyalties been so weak, party affiliations so fluid, party organizations so irrelevant.

—Arthur Schlesinger, Jr., 1973

It is painful to watch the lingering illness of an old friend, particularly a close friend. It is equally painful to watch the lingering illness of a political institution, particularly one that has enriched our history and helped make our govern-

229

ment processes manageable. Yet we have been watching the slow and agonizing decline of our parties over the past few decades, both as organizations capable of permitting Americans to contribute a sense of perspective and balance to our political life, and as meaningful entities within the consciousness of the American voter. Clinton Rossiter's confidence in the ability of the two major parties to continue functioning effectively has been replaced by Arthur Schlesinger, Jr.'s, warning that there was less to fear from the formation of new parties than the increasing irrelevance of the old ones.

The American political party had always occupied an anomalous position in our governmental framework. Not anticipated by the framers of the Constitution, the parties began to develop in the 1790s as a response to emerging political and economic developments in the new nation. As the economic and social base of the United States changed throughout the nineteenth century, political parties came and went, largely representing regional and economic interests, and usually functioning solely as vehicles for the nomination of Presidential candidates. The decentralized structure of the American political party for nearly two hundred years has sharply contrasted with the European and Canadian models of a unitary, national party whose members in parliament are tied closely by organization and policy to the party's national structure and rank-and-file membership.

The President and the Parties

As the two principal parties now remaining in our system emerged in the mid-nineteenth century, they shared a decentralized, federalized nature. The Democratic and Republican parties came to be more collections of state and local party interests—often with very differing ideological positions—rather than national parties with coherent platforms and strong national leadership. Yet for decades in the late nineteenth and early twentieth centuries, the parties had been powerful in spite of their structural weaknesses. They performed valuable social welfare functions on the local level, particularly during the period in which masses of new immigrants inundated the United States. In an era before the existence of a civil service system, they performed an important employment function for thousands of patronage jobs. And they brought out the vote, often overlooking the niceties of principle in exchange for post-victory patronage.

But in recent years, the role of parties in our political system has steadily changed. No one argues that parties exert the same influence they did a half-century ago, and only a few argue that they should. Their passage into ill health, in fact, has gone largely unlamented by the public as a whole, and their further deterioration into total impotence may go unmourned altogether except for a few party activists, political scientists and perceptive analysts like David Broder.

The question is, should be we concerned about this decline

and attempt to reverse it? Are parties really important, are they essential to our democratic processes? I believe very strongly that they are. For all their faults, political parties remain the most available and effective vehicles for the average American to influence public policy. One needn't be wealthy or powerful to participate in a party and to influence its direction; one need only have strongly held convictions, a determination to work hard, and an ability to persuade others. Thousands of individuals combined these qualities in 1968 and succeeded in fundamentally changing Democratic—and American—policy in Vietnam. Many individual Republicans similarly influenced their party's reaction to Watergate. And less visibly, thousands of individuals in both parties affect public policies on the state and local level virtually every day.

There is a growing feeling of powerlessness in America, a feeling that large public and private institutions which influence our daily lives cannot in turn be influenced by the individual citizen. Communication in our society, many believe, is only one way—from the top down. We hear our elected officials speaking to us on radio and television, but we can't effectively speak to them. It is an increasingly common refrain, and an increasingly frustrating one. Political parties don't offer a complete answer to this frustration, but they are perhaps the best single answer available. They are still the most effective mass organizations for communicating views upwards in our society, although regrettably too much of that effectiveness remains unrealized.

Parties can and should serve other vital functions as well. They are an essential instrument in keeping elected officials politically accountable. They offer one of the best counterforces to special interests. They can provide new candidates and new ideas when old ones prove ineffective or unacceptable. Perhaps most importantly, they can help formulate public policy and then see that it is implemented, not for the sake of narrow partisanship, because that is a specious basis for any policy, but rather in a way that is based on party principle, popular opinion and the public interest.

Political parties, in short, can be one of the healthiest influences in our political process if they are strengthened and revitalized in such a way that their full potential can be realized. But before prescribing a cure for the ailing patient, it is first necessary to diagnose and understand the causes of its failing health.

The decline of party influence in our political life is a complex development. The turning point, however, probably came with the New Deal. Ever since the Franklin Roosevelt adminstration, when many of the social welfare functions previously performed by the parties were taken over by the federal government, much of the parties' local base has been eroded. Patronage decreased through the broadening of civil service, and as the American electorate became increasingly educated and sophisticated, party ties were loosened as voters paid less attention to party labels.

Perhaps most importantly, the age of television had a revolutionary impact on the "merchandizing" of candidates. Television enabled the candidate to appeal directly to the voting public, without use of the party; it enabled him to personalize his campaigns, to finance them through his own organizations, and to use the newly developing techniques of voter analysis and apolitical campaign management without resorting to the old party structure. These changes affected all the functions of the party in electing candidates on the local and state level, as well as on the national level; but this change was most dramatic in affecting the party's role in the election of our Presidents.

Many have observed that there are really no national parties in America, and that what really exists are a multitude of state and local parties which coalesce every four years in the most important expression of a party's function—the nomination and election of a President. Yet with the arrival of television and the computer, of apolitical campaign management and an increasingly educated electorate, this crucial function had been transformed. The signs of party decline are clear. A Gallup poll conducted in 1968 indicated that 84 percent of those polled said they would choose the person and not the party in selecting a President. The increase in ticket-splitting has been enormous in recent elections. The percentage of congressional districts in which a President of one party and a congressman of another party were chosen fluctuated from under 5 percent in 1920 to a peak of just over 20 percent in 1948. Since then, however, there has been a dramatic change. In the Presidential election of 1956, the percentage of ticket-splitting climbed above 30 percent, by 1964, to 35 percent, and by 1972, to a remarkable 45 percent.

And while the precise implications of these shifts may not all yet be apparent, the general trend of recent years is unmistakable. Survey work done by the University of Michigan Research Center since 1948 indicates that before 1964, party identification was the single most important factor in making voting decisions, while the platforms of the parties' candidates were distinctly less important. Since 1964, however, voters have become more interested in issues and less interested in party affiliation.

Whether in fact this trend began in 1964 with the ideological polarization of the Johnson-Goldwater election, or in the 1950s with the Eisenhower Presidency, which sought to be above politics and appeal to a bipartisan constituency, or even with the similar appeals of Franklin Roosevelt in the early New Deal, is not entirely clear. Whenever the trend began, its culmination in terms of Presidential politics was reached in 1972, when Richard Nixon ran his campaign as if the Republican Party did not exist. Bob Dole, 1972 GOP chairman, was asked whether the Republican Party had been involved in Watergate. He replied that not only was the party not involved in Watergate, but it was not involved in the nomination, the campaign, the election or the inauguration of Richard Nixon.

The Presidency of Richard Nixon carried the separation of President from party to its ultimate conclusion. The 1972 campaign marked the victory of a President who chose to isolate himself from his party and run on his own. In fact, he not only isolated himself from the Republican Party but actually seemed intent on preventing the party from benefiting from—and thereby perhaps weakening—the enormous political advantage he then held. As GOP activist Kevin Phillips has remarked, "In 1972, the White House clique—selfish, political amateurs to the end—waged virtual war on Republican Party regulars, refusing to help local GOP candidates and showing no interest in the future of the rest of the party." The deliberate attempt of the Nixon people to separate, in the voters' minds, the identification of President and party was made explicitly clear in the name of his campaign committee—the Committee to Re-elect the President—and in the nonparty make-up of its leadership.

Never before had a President been so removed from the influence of his party, and the dangers of such a split became tragically clear as Watergate unraveled. A President out of touch with party politics is a President who feels no accountability to the men and women who are close to the reality of political life. Such a President has severed one more essential link in maintaining the sense of perspective which is vital for the effective functioning of the Presidential office and the achievement of restraint on arbitrary Presidential action.

When Richard Nixon summarily fired Archibald Cox, when he failed to comply with the subpoenas of the House Judiciary Committee, when he seriously considered resisting the order of the Supreme Court to turn over Watergate-related tapes and documents, the dangers of a Presidency without party ties were clearly revealed. These were actions taken without any consultation with party leaders; indeed, they defied the considered judgment of many within the Republican Party.

Mr. Nixon pursued a course in which he knowingly jeopardized the future of his own political party and many Republicans in Congress in pursuit of his own survival. When he was asked at a news conference in March 1974 whether he would continue to resist resigning even if failure to do so would damage his party, he replied that "I want my party to succeed, but more important, I want the Presidency to survive, and it is vitally important in this nation that the Presidency of the United States not be hostage to what happens to the popularity of a President at one time or another." The message was clear: Richard Nixon came first, and everything else, including the Republican Party, a distant second.

The congressional elections of 1974 are eloquent testimony to the devastation done to his party by Richard Nixon's obsession with his own self-preservation. Had the President felt any obligation to his party, he might have followed a different course, thereby avoiding the tragic end of his Presidency and the severe strains on our democratic system.

Yet Richard Nixon was not the first to work outside his party. President Eisenhower, a former soldier who came late to political life, had a deep distaste for partisan political activity. As he said in 1954, "I think it is quite apparent that I am not very much a partisan. Times are too serious, I think, to indulge in partisanship to the extreme."

All recent Presidents seem to have treated their national parties with benign neglect and sometimes with contempt. Though there were those, particularly around President Kennedy, who did want to strengthen the national party, the impact of all these recent Presidencies was to weaken their national parties. This tendency was occasionally encouraged by White House staffs which often viewed independent power centers in their parties as a threat to their own influence.

Recent Presidents, desiring to dominate the political scene, have often bypassed their parties and thus undermined their capacity for serious resistance to Presidential policies. This tendency, combined with other factors contributing to the progressive decay of the parties as influential institutions, have helped produce a number of unhealthy trends.

The President and the Parties

Presidential campaigns have become successively less tied to their parties, and more to the personalities and organizations of individual candidates. This overpersonalization of Presidential campaigns, as discussed earlier, helped lead to the abuses of CREEP in the 1972 Nixon campaign. And more generally, it has resulted in the inability of parties—which have a continuing stake in their credibility with the electorate—to retain any substantial degree of influence in the campaigns of their Presidential nominees.

Unfortunately, the Federal Election Campaign Act of 1974 will not help reverse this trend; indeed, it may accelerate it by decreasing the party's traditional role in the important area of fund-raising. Now, aided by radio and television, Presidential candidates can go directly to the people, largely ignoring their political parties. By removing the indebtedness of a candidate to his party, this Act leaves less reason for the candidates to be accountable to their parties. And while the reforms in our campaign finance system were essential to avoid the compromise and even corruption stemming from the old system of campaign finance, we cannot ignore the potentially serious implications for further erosion of the influence of political parties. There are some who disagree that public financing will have such an effect on the parties on the ground that they never played a large role in financing Presidential campaigns. Indeed, the degree of that role has varied substantially from time to time and recently it has been more of a potential party function than a fulfilled one. Even so, financing reforms have seriously lessened the opportunities for close campaign ties between a Presidential candidate and his party and thus weakened another opportunity for accountability.

Once a President has been nominated and elected, he simply does not need political parties for very much anymore. One interesting measure of this fact is the strange but consistent tendency of recent Presidents to go outside the party political structure in picking individuals to fill key administration positions. Too often the Adlai Stevensons and the Chester Bowles who have had close party ties have been bypassed in favor of the Dean Rusks and Robert McNamaras, and later the Henry Kissingers and James Schlesingers, who have had few, if any, party ties.

Once in office, our greatest leaders often seem to distrust their own party's leadership, perhaps once again in an attempt to minimize the partisan appearance of a new administration. The goal—particularly in foreign affairs—has often been to remove the constraints of partisan politics by appealing to both parties for cooperation in formulating policies on which substantial differences are supposed to vanish because of "national security." I once asked a top government official how long a democratic society could fight a foreign war that was bitterly tearing apart not only the administration's party but the country as well. He responded, "Its about time the Democratic Party pulled up its socks."

We also seem to have lost much of the ability of the party out of power to articulate comprehensive and relevant party positions on the crucial issues. During the 1950s, through a body under the leadership of Stephen Mitchell and Paul Butler, the Democratic Party was able to enunciate national policy positions on a variety of issues. While this so-called Democratic Advisory Council was not totally representative of the Democratic Party, it did have status as the official policy-making body of the party. This, in addition to the status of its members, lent substantial weight to its policy positions. By issuing "state of the union" messages and adopting policy positions in a dozen fields, the advisory council served as a counterforce to Democratic congressional leadership which was often bent on compromise even if that required a blurring of the Democratic Party's position.

This type of strong and consistent party voice has been lacking within both parties for over a decade. And while the influence of personalities is obviously a factor, the inability of the party out of power to formulate positions on the central issues facing the nation has helped remove one important restraint on recent Presidents. Particularly if the party out of power controls the Congress, as has been true in the Eisenhower, Nixon and Ford administrations, that party must conduct a vigorous opposition debate on the crucial questions of foreign and domestic policy if Presidents are to be held accountable.

Democratic National Chairman Bob Strauss has attempted to meet this need by resurrecting the advisory council concept of the fifties in the form of the Democratic Advisory Council of Elected Officials headed by businessman Arthur Krim. Whereas its predecessor was viewed as a rival policy-making body by the Democratic congressional leadership, thereby creating what some thought was a healthy tension between the latter and the national party, Strauss included a broadly representative number of congressmen, senators and other officials on the council. With Averell Harriman heading its foreign affairs task force and Harry McPherson its domestic task force, the council has issued a number of policy positions on economic, energy and other matters that have been a helpful stimulus to congressional action.

Finally, along with a decline in meaningful opposition by the party out of power in recent years, American party politics have suffered from the lack of institutional mechanisms within the party in power to convey the dissatisfaction of elements of the party with Presidential policy.

To be sure, some Democrats voiced strong objection to the conduct of the war in Vietnam under Lyndon Johnson, as did some Republicans to the Watergate scandal under President Nixon. And yet the absence, for example, of an institutionalized Democratic policy conference in 1966 to discuss Democratic opposition on the war in Vietnam meant that President Johnson could not accurately gauge the depth and extent of disenchantment by members of his own party with his war policy. Such a conference might have substantially affected the course of the war by giving the President a clear warning signal of rebellion within his own party.

The decline of our parties has reduced the ability for either party to influence significantly its candidates for the Presidency. It has resulted in a desire to remove the appearance of partisanship from debate on vital policy issues and in a weakening of the ability of both the party out of power and the party in power to influence Presidential actions. And for both parties, their declining health as institutions has reduced their ability to articulate meaningful positions on issues which concern Americans.

The American system is such that we will probably not see the emergence of parties in the European and Canadian style. The principal historic function of the American political party has been the nomination and election of a Presidential candidate and, because of this fact, the parties have been and will likely remain coalitions of widely divergent groups.

But the inability of our system to accommodate the style of other systems must not mean simply giving up on our parties as curious anachronisms unsuited to the realities of late-twentieth-century politics. Although the Presidential nominating process has been the principal role of the national party, it has through this process come to perform other crucially important functions. First, it helps arrive at consensus—not between parties, but within each party—to find and articulate areas of agreement on issues which matter to the people. And second, it can act as a restraint on Presidents—whether of their own party or the opposition—by keeping alive responsible partisan debate.

Both of these functions are in danger today. But despite the heavy odds working against the parties today—the power of television, the decline in party identification by the voters, and the decay of many of the traditional functions of the party—I believe there is hope that we can reach a workable, peculiarly American middle ground between consensus politics on the one hand and European-style democracy on the other.

Tempering this hope is the fact that we must be realistic in our expectations of political parties. Because they are the most unstructured and ill-defined of all our national institutions, they are the most easily manipulated by Presidents intent on ignoring or subverting them. No institutional reform of the parties will change this basic fact of life of American politics: that we are not a European-type democracy, and that we can expect only so much from our national parties.

And yet at the same time that our parties seem to be in trouble, a curious and very hopeful countertrend is developing. In the last decade, while general party allegiance and identification have decreased, more and more people have chosen to become party activists. The war in Vietnam may be responsible for the increased involvement in Democratic Party affairs. But even after the war's effects were over, the surge in party involvement remained. In Minnesota alone, for example, Democratic precinct caucus attendance has risen from below 40,000 to over 100,000 in the last decade, and the Republican figures show an almost similar increase. This means that in a state of under 4 million people, nearly 200,000 people from both parties attend approximately 8,000 precinct caucuses around the state in a single evening.

Increased party involvement is not unique to Minnesota. It has occurred throughout the United States, and the challenge we face is harnessing the energies of these political participants in a way which will enable us to build a stronger national party better able to hold Presidents accountable. Ironically, the same increase in voter interest in substantive issues over the past decade—which accompanied the decline of party identification—can now be used as a means for once again increasing the viability of the two-party system. The aim is not to replace a healthy interest in issues with a blind obedience to the party but rather to strengthen the role of the party in the minds of the electorate as taking significant positions on the issues which will dominate voter concern for the foreseeable future.

Such issues as economic health and prosperity, energy shortages and security of supply, foreign policy, health care, and the continuing debate over national priorities will inevitably dominate our political scene for years to come. And as these issues dominate our politics, the role of the parties can once again gain greater meaning in helping to define and articulate positions over which future elections will be fought. To be sure, neither party will achieve a unanimity of approach to each of these pressing problems; but both should strive for as much cohesiveness as possible. Above all, both parties must avoid adding the insult of a "bipartisan" economic policy to the injuries already sustained from the decades of a "bipartisan" foreign policy. James MacGregor Burns has said that "almost as many crimes have been committed in the name of mindless bipartisanship as in the name of mindless patriotism." That warning takes on new meaning as political figures and the parties they represent tackle the maze of complex and difficult issues we face.

We need partisanship not for the sake of divisiveness but to maintain a healthy debate in our democracy and a workable system of constraints on our Presidents. We need partisanship not in every instance and not on every issue, but to aid the reestablishment, in the minds of the American voter, of the real differences over broad economic and other issues which have so often separated the two major parties. If Democrats and Republicans alike move toward the definition of party positions which are significant, our party system can regain its vitality. But if we fail to appreciate the significant role which these positions can perform in our political process, the present illness of our party system may quickly worsen.

Any further weakening of party restraints on our Presidents can only help prolong and strengthen the lack of accountability within our democracy which has taken its costly toll over the past decade. Obviously, we do not want—nor are we likely ever to have—Presidents who are mere employees responding to the orders of their parties. But we urgently need Presidents who listen to party views on the important issues facing the nation.

The responsiveness of our Presidents to their parties—and to the parties out of power as well—cannot be reestablished unless the parties are themselves given new institutional life. The party structures in Congress alone cannot do the job: the strength of our parties at the local and state levels as well as at the national level, must also be renewed so that all can play an important role. Although there are clearly limits to what we can realistically expect to achieve through structural reform of our parties, there are nonetheless broad goals toward which we must work.

1. We must recognize that the Federal Election Campaign Act of 1974 may have weakened, rather than strengthened, the political parties by substantially decreasing the fund-raising function of the party. This recognition, however, must lead us to search for other means of bringing greater party involvement in national political affairs—and particu-

larly in those ways which can serve to hold Presidents more accountable for their conduct.

One major step in this direction would be the institution of regular national party policy conferences in both major parties. Our national political parties do not have policy conferences comparable to those held annually by the British, at which they adopt programs which become official party policy. Because of the differences in our political systems, the role of such policy conferences might be different in our country. Such conferences nonetheless could prove extraordinarily valuable as sounding boards for party opinion and opportunities for both the party in power and the party out of power to attempt to develop more unified national issues positions.

In December of 1974, the Democratic Midterm Convention in Kansas City narrowly defeated a proposal to include quadrennial policy conferences in the Democratic Party charter. Many of us believe, however, that this type of regularized policy conference is absolutely essential. If we have such a conference in 1978, it will be of great value, whichever party controls the White House. If the Democrats are in control, such a conference could provide the opportunity for elements within the party to voice their dissatisfaction with the way in which our President is handling important issues. If the Republicans retain control, this conference could help formulate Democratic Party responses to a Republican administration and thereby help make victory in 1980 easier.

The President and the Parties

The experience of the Kansas City mini-convention should also tell us that regular policy conferences could not only help keep Presidents accountable but serve as a healthy influence upon the Congress. The message of the Kansas City convention in adopting economic resolutions on behalf of the party was to prod the Congress—which we control—into action. This was a valuable lesson for a Democratic Congress, and another important function which policy conferences could play.

There are obviously dangers in such conferences. They could at times become more divisive than unifying. They could become rubber stamps for Presidents when such conferences are held by the party in power. And without proper input into planning and implementation of such conferences by elected officials at all levels, in addition to party activists, such conferences could factionalize more than unite the parties.

I am confident, however, that each of these potential problems can be overcome. The Kansas City Democratic conference did deal with the central economic issues facing the nation in late 1974, not with fringe issues. I doubt very strongly that—at least in the Democratic Party—any such conference would become a rubber stamp for an incumbent President, in view of the strong history of party activism. And by ensuring that local, state and national party officials are included in every stage of the planning process, we can make these policy conferences a means for accentuating party unity in a positive way. There is an enormous benefit to the party simply in bringing people together from around the country to build informal relationships so essential to the development of a truly national party. Finally, the holding of these conferences totally apart from the Presidential nominating process will permit an objective and concentrated focus on questions of party policy and organization which is not otherwise possible.

2. The policy conference by itself, of course, cannot restore the accountability of elected officials to their party. If the parties are to deal effectively with them, frankly, they will need more clout. They will need to have, in short, something the elected officials either need or want, which means, in effect, either campaign funds or campaign services. The parties can best accomplish this by developing a strong professional staff which would serve through successive administrations and which is capable of offering a high degree of expertise in direct-mail fund-raising, voter registration and turnout, campaign organization and other specialized services. This kind of capability, if institutionalized and made permanent, can become a major stabilizing influence and an increasingly strong foundation for establishing Presidential accountability to the party. The Democrats, at their Kansas City charter conference, took a major step forward in this area by establishing a National Training and Education Council, originally conceived by Congressman Donald

Fraser of Minnesota, designed to offer just this kind of expertise within the party.

3. If we are to have an established party apparatus, however, we must pay for it. And we should therefore consider amending the new campaign spending reform act to add a modest set-aside from the dollar check-off system to defray part of the cost of ongoing party operations. The Act does provide $2 million for each party's quadrennial national convention, but nothing for them between conventions.

As was done in the Campaign Finance Act, these federal funds going to the parties should be set up in a matching form, with each party required to receive a minimum number of small contributions from a number of states in order to qualify for federal funding. This would force the parties to keep in better touch with the public and would prevent the parties from becoming totally dependent on federal funds.

4. The parties must continue their efforts of recent years to build in more accountability to the party process by completing the codification of their party rules. The Democrats in particular, thanks to the leadership and persistence of Don Fraser and others, have made great progress in this direction by adopting a written party charter for the first time in American history. The Kansas City convention in December of 1974, in addition to setting out issue positions on the economic problems facing us, had as its principal job the ratification of these rules. By establishing delegate se-lection procedures, ground rules for party conventions, and a framework for greater public participation in party affairs, the Democratic rule-making process has helped give struc-ture and meaning to a previously loose group of party habits and customs. Adoption of party bylaws will complete the process.

We cannot expect too much from this attempt to bring the "rule of law" to political parties. Had there been an incum-bent Democratic President in 1974, these rules and the party charter might never have been adopted. But in fact they were, and now they will help hold Presidents and party leaders alike more accountable to these rules and procedures.

5. Because the national parties usually cannot dictate their will, the parties in Congress must continue their recent efforts to build more cohesive and influential party caucuses in the House and Senate. In recent years these caucuses have gradually developed as instruments for influencing congres-sional action. Due largely to Mike Mansfield's leadership, the Senate Democratic Conference has served as an increasingly effective party voice, particularly when it has differed with Republican administration policies. In the first vote of its kind anywhere on Capitol Hill, Senate Democrats voted in 1971 in favor of withdrawing American forces from South Vietnam. It was a major policy breakthrough even at that late date, and the Senate's position on continuing the war

was never in doubt thereafter. The Senate
Conference subsequently adopted a number of
tions on energy, the economy and a host of other
many of these later became the subject of full S

Democratic caucuses in both Houses profou
congressional procedures by voting to open
meetings to the public, and to require committ
to submit to a secret caucus ballot at the begin
Congress in order to maintain their chairmansl
instituting a number of other reforms design
about greater openness and accountability with
gress. The Republican caucuses have been less ac
areas than their Democratic counterparts so far, l
are showing increasing signs of forging policy-
struments out of their House and Senate member

We must continue to strengthen the cohesiver
party caucuses just as much as the intraparty
within the congressional parties will permit.
consequences of the absence of effective restraint
Presidents by either their own parties or the
highlights the need for renewed attempts to fash
ments within the Congress, as well as outside it,
seriously discuss issues and take positions with a vi
a significant party role in legislation.

6. The national parties have a unique opportuni
rationality and a national approach to a Preside
inating process which presently lacks both. As

earlier, the Supreme Court, in *Cousins* v. *Wigoda*, declared that national parties can establish their own rules for the selection of delegates to their national conventions, even if those rules conflict with state law. Too little attention has been paid to this far-reaching decision and the opportunity it affords the parties, but it's hard to imagine anything they might do to reestablish their credibility, vitality and clout more than overhauling the nominating process.

In one of the first speeches of his campaign for the Presidential nomination, John Kennedy said:

> No President can escape politics. He has not wholly been chosen by the nation, he has been chosen by his party, and if he insists that he is the President of all the people, and should therefore offend none of them, if he blurs the issues and differences between the two parties, if he neglects the party machinery and avoids his party's leadership, then he has not only weakened the political party as an instrument of the democratic process, he has dealt a blow to the democratic process itself.

No President—including John Kennedy—has ever truly reached this ideal: Presidential leadership which continually recognizes the role of strengthening and consulting the party in the exercise of that leadership. Certainly no President will

ever reach that ideal so long as the parties themselves do not become forces with which Presidents must contend. And while we cannot expect too much from our political parties, neither should we be satisfied with accepting their current state of weakness.

We are not likely to have parties that dictate to Presidents. But we do need parties which are perceived by Presidents as being full participants in the governmental process. And when this perception becomes a reality, another cornerstone of Presidential accountability will have been restored.

10

The Presidential
Personality and
Public Leadership

*My God, what is there in this place that a man should ever want to
get in it.*
—*President James Garfield*

*No President ever enjoyed himself in the Presidency as much as I did.
And no President ever leaving office took as much joy in life as I am
taking.*
—*President Theodore Roosevelt*

*Governments are what politicians make them. Government is not a
body of blind forces but a body of men—not a machine, but a living
thing. It falls not under the theory of the universe, but under the
theory of organic life. It is accountable to Darwin, not to Newton.*
—*President Woodrow Wilson*

For as long as there has been an American Presidency, there
has been a debate over the relative importance of institutions
and personalities in shaping the office. The Presidency is a
malleable instutition. It can be shaped by institutional
change, or by the swifter and less predictable impact of

256

different Presidents, or both. Obviously, both factors are crucial. The institutional forces which help shape the Presidency are complex and changing. And the imprint of Presidential personalities on the institutions surrounding the office is strong and compelling.

Indeed, the role of Presidential personality has helped mold the institution of the Presidency since its creation. Pierce Butler, a delegate to the Constitutional Convention, wrote in 1788 that he did not believe that the executive powers conferred by the delegates on the President would have been so great "had not many of the members cast their eyes toward General Washington as President; and shaped their Ideas of the Powers to be given a President, by the opinions of his Virtue." If the virtues of a George Washington helped give the Presidency the powers it was to receive in the Constitution, the office which he helped shape in turn left its imprint on his personality. After seven years of governing the new nation, Washington could write to Henry Knox in March of 1794, comparing himself "to the wearied traveller, who sees a resting-place and is bending his body to lean thereon," and lamenting the attempts "to misrepresent my motives, to reprobate my politics, and to weaken the confidence which has been reposed in my administration" by those "who will be satisfied with nothing short of a change in our political system." The impact of governing had left its mark on Washington, just as he had helped impress the institution he occupied by the force of his personality.

Two hundred years later, another particularly important meeting of institutions and personalities occurred with the inauguration of Richard Nixon. As Arthur Schlesinger, Jr., noted:

> With Nixon there came, whether by weird historical accident or by unconscious national response to historical pressure and possibility, a singular confluence of the job with the man. The Presidency, as enlarged by international delusions and domestic propulsions, found a President whose inner mix of vulnerability and ambition impelled him to push the historical logic to its extremity.

Just as the new nation had drawn strength and passed through a period of crisis aided by the personality of George Washington, so the mature America of the 1970s was deeply shaken by the excesses of the Nixon administration. Pursuing a strategy of unprecedented arrogation of Presidential power only timidly resisted by the institutions empowered to do so, surrounded by men who shared with him a contempt for the democratic process, and convinced of his own righteousness, President Nixon and his men, in Senator Lowell Weicker's words, "almost stole America."

In the wake of the Nixon Presidency, the American people have taken a renewed and serious interest in the personal makeup of Presidential candidates. A healthy President must be capable of earning the trust of the American people. He can do so only if he tells the truth, obeys the law, and respects the American public and their right to an accounting of his leadership. Such a President will reject what some have called the "paranoid school" of American politics, and under such leadership the chances of another Watergate should diminish.

Americans now want to know whether politicians have a healthy perspective on the world and on themselves; whether they have bloated egos capable of further distortion; whether they will remember that the people put them in office and that they bear a responsibility to them. They want to know a politician's record. Does he or she have a record that shows respect for the law and a willingness to accept defeat if need be rather than break or subvert the law? Does that record show a fundamental respect for the civil liberties of the American people guaranteed under the Bill of Rights? Do their personalities and careers show that they have told the truth even in times of difficulty, and that they have demanded the same from those working for them?

I am quite convinced that we must look very closely into a candidate's sense of humor and sense of proportion. I campaigned for over a year seeking the Presidency. The tremendous pressure and incredible schedules and fatigue and everything else that goes into a national campaign must be experienced to be believed. It takes an extraordinary or remarkable person to go through all that is necessary. And yet that very pressure and demanding schedule may be the most crucial test of one's ability to make a good President.

A Presidential campaign requires a candidate to speak throughout the nation, to listen carefully, and to learn about the problems of regions and communities. All of this is an essential part of the education of potential Presidents about this country. I think only candidates can realize how incredibly vast and varied America is. It is only this way that candidates can become familiar with this country, with its people and their leaders, with its problems. In this way, they can come to respect the differences that exist in our country. And through this educational process a truly national leader, capable of dealing intelligently, responsibly and respectfully with our nation's problems, can be developed.

When I withdrew from the Presidential race, I indicated that I simply did not have the overwhelming desire necessary to do what had to be done to be elected. Many took this to mean that I did not believe it would be possible for a person to seek the Presidency successfully who did not have an obsession so great as to raise serious questions about his mental health. I feel very strongly that this need not be the case, as I tried to express in my statement of withdrawal.

In fact, I think many candidates have healthy mental attitudes. Politics did not ruin Richard Nixon. Richard Nixon almost ruined politics. My colleague, Hubert Humphrey, has sought the Presidency vigorously and with great energy, but he has been able to do so while keeping a perfectly healthy attitude. Ambition is essential to anyone who seeks the Presidency, and obviously one must have a very strong ambition to go through what is needed. But that doesn't mean that a successful candidate must be mentally ill. I am convinced that the crucial element is one's ability to enjoy and appreciate politics, to enjoy being with people, to sustain a sense of excitement and even celebration over the task of participating in democratic decision-making and leadership.

People are extraordinarly kind, respectful and supportive. They appreciate and know what you are going through. They sustain and buoy you. Almost always, they strengthen one's conviction of the basic validity of a political system which is founded upon a trust and appreciation of people and their judgment. I have served my state for many years and I sought the Presidency for a long time. During this time, I have seen every day and every hour people intelligently searching and worrying and concerning themselves about their communities and their country. And through this I have come to more fully admire and appreciate our system, the quality and concern of our people, and to recognize the privilege and joy of living in our country and being permitted to participate in our remarkable democracy. There is no reason, in my opinion, why a candidate viewing politics in this light cannot gain strength and a sense of fulfillment and have great fun in the practice of politics and Presidential leadership. John Adams once said that "the happiness of society is the end of government." I believe we must seek leadership that views its task in that light.

And I believe the American people are beginning again to see this need. The public now realizes that we need Presidents who can ask questions without being ashamed; who can develop new approaches without being isolated; who can provide leadership without being dictatorial. The American people have seen the dangers of the politics of paranoia and vengeance. They now appreciate the peril of allowing government to be run with a siege mentality which views openness and accountability as objects of fear, and which believes that its principal goal is the destruction of its political enemies.

The American people have seen that the Presidency is far too important an office to be occupied by individuals who view vengeance, rather than compassion; retribution, rather than restoration; as their paths to political glory. We do not need messiahs pitting North against South or black against white, but rather leaders who will bring forth the qualities of compassion and justice which the American people have always possessed.

A Presidential candidate's career and personality are crucially important in our search for a more accountable Presidency. Presidents whose personalities and backgrounds show a love of politics in the best sense of the word, a desire to be with people and a respect for the intelligence and decency of the American public are far less likely to resort to illegality

262

when in the Presidency. Presidents who have an understanding of the principal problems facing the country and the world and who have a similar understanding of the need for compassion in dealing with those problems are far less likely to fail our nation at crucial times in our history.

Presidents who have a sense of humility, who recognize, as Judge Learned Hand once remarked, that "the spirit of liberty is the spirit which is not too sure that it is right" are much less likely to overstep the proper bounds of Presidential power.

Political leaders do not appear on the Presidential scene without political track records. Those records demonstrate their philosophy and conduct over the years. Richard Nixon's record was clear—as Jerry Voorhees, Helen Gahagan Douglas or the newsmen who attened his 1962 "last" news conference will confirm. We had clear evidence about his personality and methods. The California court which judged his campaign organization guilty of violations of election laws in 1962 should have helped make that obvious.

We should have had severe doubts that any politician who did so much to show his contempt for fairness and truth and the American people, and did so while in his mature years, could somehow be reborn and no longer resort to such tactics.

All the warning signals in the world will do no good, however, unless the American public is given access to them and takes them seriously. And just as we must be on guard against the bad, so we must be able to distinguish the good in our potential Presidents' character.

One of our foremost scholars on the Presidential personality, James David Barber, has warned us that we will have missed much of the lesson of the past decade unless we look not only to honesty and decency but also to the fitness of Presidents to exploit the positive possibilities of the Presidency and to the beliefs and character of future Presidents. This means studying the past to determine not only a candidate's position on issues but also his concept of the government's role in the lives of Americans. It means probing a candidate's sense of himself as well as his sense of the public's needs; determining whether he seeks the Presidency for fear the nation will fall into ruin without his leadership or whether he maintains a sense of perspective about the ability of the nation to survive without him as Chief Executive.

Our Presidents must also bring to the office a sense of the excitement over the achievements possible through the responsible exercise of Presidential power. Ralph Waldo Emerson once said that "every great and commanding moment in the annals of the world is the triumph of some enthusiasm." This enthusiasm should be a part of our President's view of his job, and it should help him to keep a needed perspective as he performs it.

We have always realized the role of personality and character in shaping the nature of the Presidency. Now,

264

however, we know the result of failing to give them the highest attention in choosing our Presidents.

The evaluation of the character and personality of Presidential candidates is not simple. The media's responsibility in analyzing the platforms of those who want to be President and the way their past and present actions reflect their likely conduct if elected to the White House is obvious. As Barber observes:

> If that means journalists must make judgments about human responses—even psychological judgments—so be it. For the best are and long have been in that business. For better or worse, anyone who wants to make sense of once or future Presidents must look past the events of the day to the experiences of the life, and try to gauge the pattern and rhythm of it.

If the roles of the media—and the political parties as well—are important in gauging Presidential character, the role of the American people in converting this information into an electoral choice is most important. The excesses of the past decade have made the American public more wary of politicians, but in the process it has also made them more willing to ask the rough questions about character which go far toward determining the effectiveness and accountability of a President. But there is clearly a danger that as the memories of Vietnam and Watergate fade, we will once again fail to pay adequate attention to the need for both strong leadership potential and strong moral character.

The task is to combine a search for qualities of leadership and qualities of honesty which, taken together, may yield a vigorous but responsible Presidency. And while the will of the American people to make this search—aided by the media and the parties—must be present in order for that search to succeed, the people must have the information on which to base a sound judgment.

Because of this need, we encounter one of those ironies that so frequently seems to characterize the Presidency and our governmental institutions. For in order to better evaluate the personalities of our future Presidents, structural reforms will be required to make this evaluation process more meaningful. Even as those who insist that institutions are incapable of improving the chances for Presidential accountability feel the need for placing more emphasis on personalities, so they must recognize that the present institutional arrangements of our political campaigns simply do not afford the people an adequate opportunity to test the character of their Presidents.

The most dramatic failure of our present system is the ability of Presidential candidates to avoid contact with their opponents and with the people through the advertising power inherent in a Nixonesque use of the electronic media.

266

The Presidential Personality

I have earlier discussed the need for a system which would guarantee the type of televised Presidential debates which we have seen only once before, in 1960. By giving our major party candidates the mechanism through which to demand frequent debates during any Presidential campaign, this system will do more than simply allow the public to ascertain where the candidates stand on crucial issues. For if the experience of 1960 is relevant, it will also help the public understand more about the character of those seeking the Presidential office. Richard Nixon lost ground, and John Kennedy gained support, in the 1960 debates not because of a poor makeup job or an ill-fitting suit, but rather because by seeing the contrasting styles of Nixon and Kennedy the people could better gauge the way these men viewed themselves and the world. This is the value of television debates: to open to public scrutiny candidates who can otherwise isolate themselves through the controlled use of campaign television. Unless these opportunities to evaluate candidates occur with greater regularity, there is little chance that Americans can have the opportunity to know more about the Presidents they choose—before it is too late.

Not only should we demand that candidates debate but the media must insist that candidates present themselves for thorough questioning. And if candidates refuse to do so, there must be a remedy by diminishing the media's coverage of materials candidates seek to present to the American people without critical analysis.

267

There is a similar need to preserve and strengthen the present mixed primary and convention system. Some believe that the choices made by the voters in eliminating all but one candidate to represent each of the major parties is a more important process than the general election process itself. In the preconvention months, the philosophies of differing candidates *can* be examined, often at rather close ranges, because of a system that puts a premium on contact with the people. Certainly, many of the strains of the primary system have their undesirable side effects; but the requirement that candidates face their opposition state by state is a healthy one.

And not only the primary system itself but the entire mixed system of primaries, precinct caucuses and state conventions is important. Through many of the nonprimary procedures, those involved in party affairs can come to know the people seeking the Presidency. They can evaluate their character, their integrity and their willingness to exercise accountable power. Consequently, the responsibility of these party people is a heavy one which must be fully exercised if we are to get a full examination of our Presidential candidates.

Anything that increases the public's view of its Presidential candidates and its Presidents in meaningful ways should be encouraged—be it televised debates, or a vigorous primary and convention system, or frequent news conferences, or more media attention to character and personality. Each is not without its risks for exploitation and distortion; but together, these types of opportunities to learn more about Presidential character can help both in opening up the Presidency and placing in that office individuals whose personalities are more hospitable to the exercise of accountable power.

This greater public scrutiny of the personalities and characters of our Presidents must be coupled with increasing attention to the need for institutional reform. The institutions I have discussed—including the Congress, the parties and the media—each have a role to play in making Presidential conduct more responsive to democratic ideals.

These institutions in our society will be required to keep up the pressure that results in both institutional and psychological restraints on the exercise of unaccountable Presidential power. The potential for disaster in the Presidential office is as great as the potential for achievement, and unless Presidents are continually confronted with the political price of abusing their power, that disaster may once again become a reality.

Certainly, based on our history, we cannot assume that any future President will resist the pressures to abandon accountable leadership without the vigilant and strong challenge of our competing public and private institutions. Many of the conditions I have described and the changes I have advocated express my belief that this accountability will be restored only if responsiveness is generated in the

Presidential personality through a greater awareness on his part of competing institutions capable of relating to him from positions of strength.

The object of many of these changes is the same, whether it is the question-and-report period or more vigilant oversight by Congress or the increased use by Congress of radio and television or the provision for televised debates during Presidential campaigns. Each has an overriding purpose: to require the President to face the public and to force the President to recognize the right and ability of that public to exercise power to restrain his conduct should he move outside the Constitution or contrary to their wishes.

This is the meaning of an open and accountable Presidency. Openness does not require a President to show the scars on his abdomen but to candidly tell the people the truth about his policies. Accountability is measured less by whether a President cooks his own breakfast than by whether he consults widely before making crucial decisions. The surface actions *are* important, because they can indicate Presidential personalities less likely to become isolated by the trappings of the Presidential establishment. But ways of thinking and perceptions of reality are more important, for they influence the types of decisions Presidents make and the kinds of policies they pursue.

To an important extent, we can legislate certain types of changes that will help increase Presidential accountability. We can legislate changes in our institutions, which can help increase Presidential awareness of the competition he must

face in the exercise of his powers. We can legislate changes
in the public access to information to lessen secrecy and
unresponsiveness. But we cannot legislate a fundamental
regard for the intelligence of the American people. We
cannot legislate greater Presidential involvement with the
Congress or the public.

These must come largely from within the Presidential
personality. Changes in institutions can help define the
boundaries of Presidential actions, but only the President
himself will ultimately determine the quality of those
actions.

We are thrown back to the interaction of personalities
and institutions which determines the effectiveness and
accountability of the Presidency. Both must be compatible
with democratic goals.

Whatever the abuses of the past, Presidential leadership
should and will continue to play an extraordinarily important—indeed, often a dominant—role in our nation's life. We
cannot forget the dynamic and usually constructive force of
Presidential leadership in shaping our history.

Without vigorous Presidential leadership, the America of
1975 would not be the strong nation it is today. As Arthur
Schlesinger, Jr., has observed:

> It was Presidential leadership, after all, that brought
> the country into the twentieth century, that civilized
> American industry, secured the rights of labor organi-

zations, defended the livelihood of the farmer. It was Presidential leadership that protected the Bill of Rights against local vigilantism and natural resources against local greed. It was Presidential leadership, spurred on by the Supreme Court, that sought to vindicate racial justice against local bigotry. Congress would have done few of these things on its own; local government even fewer.

The problems we face, in spite of the progress we have made, are enormous. These problems of equity in our economic policy, of justice and inequality, of morality and honesty in government, of the domination of large and impersonal institutions over American life, and of the need for a responsible foreign policy must be confronted. And in spite of the excesses of the past, I firmly believe that the Presidency must continue to be the central platform from which these crucial issues are discussed.

In 1932, Franklin Roosevelt defined the office of the Presidency as being "preeminently a place of moral leadership. All our great Presidents were leaders of thought at times when certain historic ideas in the life of the nation had to be clarified." We are in such a time now, and the Presidency must be directed at providing national leadership. More important, the role of the President as the voice for the powerless in our society must be reasserted with a new sense of commitment.

The Presidential Personality

We now know that in an age of large and depersonalized institutions, powerlessness is not only the burden of the poor and the minorities. It is also the lot of working men and women who are angered and confused by the decline of moral values in government and the inability of that government to respond to their most basic needs. We suffer from alienation in the midst of affluence, a disintegration of the concepts of political honesty and morality, and a decline in the quality of life of many Americans today.

These are difficult issues to face, must less to solve. But unless our Presidents confront these issues squarely, there is little hope for making the Presidential office vital and for moving toward the solution of the domestic and international problems we face. While we must have continuing Presidential attention to the critical problems of international affairs, our Presidents must avoid the attraction of escaping from the often more difficult domestic issues into the more glamorous world of foreign policy. Our Presidents must be willing to risk their popularity in providing leadership on these issues of crucial domestic importance. For these are the issues that often can be more open to public scrutiny and debate in their resolution, thereby increasing the public's participation in the democratic process.

There must be a fundamental difference, however, in the *manner* in which Presidential leadership is now exercised. Because of the many achievements of past Presidential leadership, we have all too often expected too much of our

Presidents. We have asked them to do the impossible, and then wondered why they failed. We have given them power without requiring accountability, and then wondered why they abused it. We have allowed the decay of other institutions surrounding the Presidency, and then wondered why Presidents have ignored them. We have too often concentrated on the achievements of Presidential leadership in the past while ignoring the problems presented by the way in which that leadership was exercised.

Now we must couple a commitment to seek responsible change with an equally strong commitment to require accountability in the process by which that change is brought about. And we must recognize that no one—including our President—possesses the answers to all our problems or the key to all our wisdom. The Congress in particular must take responsibility not only for helping restrain arbitrary Presidential conduct but also for developing the types of policy alternatives which reaffirm its central role in moving the nation toward the solution of the problems we face. The relationship between the Congress and the President, while recognizing the important role of Presidential leadership, must become one more of mutual respect among equals, with the creative potential of the Congress given fuller opportunities to develop.

To do this, our perception not only of our Presidents but also of the institutions around them must be transformed. If the Congress, the political parties, the Cabinet and the media perform their functions in helping to reshape the Presidential perspective, we will have greatly reduced the chances of a recurrence of the Presidential abuse of power. Congress is of central importance if these changes in institutional and psychological perspectives are to be meaningful. Indeed, a change in the congressional perspective is as vital as—and can be a cause of—a change in the Presidential perspective. The American people must demand more of their Congress if we are to restore a sense of balance in the exercise of governmental power.

We gain little by romanticizing the Congress in the wake of a deep national disillusionment with the Presidency. But there is great value in stressing both the vital function of the Congress in restraining unaccountable Presidential conduct and the equally important need for congressional initiatives if Presidential leadership is lacking or inadequate. To achieve this greater congressional check on arbitrary Presidential power and a reassertion of positive congressional activity in meeting pressing concerns we will need a reassertion of institutional prerogatives and a reassertion of congressional will. This process has begun, but it must be sustained and enhanced. And most importantly, just as reform of the Presidency must attempt to bring the institution closer to the people, so reform of the Congress must seek precisely the same end. As Elizabeth Drew has commented, "Congress need not establish a Pentagon on the Hill to rival the one across the Potomac. It need not replicate the federal bureaucracy. It need only have the interest and give itself the capacity to ask the right questions." If both the Presidency and the Congress become more remote from their constituencies, the future of American democracy is bleak indeed. We must recognize instead that just as every problem *may* ultimately have a solution, the means of achieving those solutions will not be easy, or quickly forthcoming, and we must rely heavily on the good sense of the American people.

The final restraint on the actions of an unaccountable Presidency and an unresponsive government can only come through the vigilance of the American people. They must define the goals our Presidents seek and set the standards on the ways in which those goals are being sought. Political leaders—and particularly our Presidents—must encourage close scrutiny; indeed, they must insist upon it. We have learned that most government secrets are far safer with the American people than with those who would keep those secrets from them. And Vietnam and Watergate have taught us that the government which seeks to achieve what it believes to be its mandate through deception, secrecy and illegality both distorts that mandate and destroys the confidence of the people in their government.

As the head of government, the President must set the standard of establishing the essential accountability of power without which the people's confidence cannot be restored. This accountability can only thrive on an active, honest relationship between a strong President, a determined Congress and an informed and concerned American people. It needs the constant test of political reality: the clash of opinions, in full view of the American public, which must mark effective dialogue in a democracy.

This is the openness which creates strength for the office of the Presidency, without inviting the abuse of that strength. This is the candor which breeds respect for the head of our government, without weakening the responsiveness of that government by turning respect into reverence. But this relationship between the people and their government can only come from a sense of trust felt by the American people. This trust can only exist when the people believe that the President is open in his dealings and accountable for his actions. And this trust must be earned.

I believe, with Harry Truman, that "there is far more good than evil in men and that it is the business of government to make the good prevail." The American people are a compassionate, humane and intelligent people, eager to meet the difficult problems facing our nation here and abroad in a spirit of justice and equity. This is the spirit in which the Presidency must be used to develop responsible leadership that respects the American people and the government under which they have prospered for nearly two centuries.

Our experiment in government has been a uniquely successful one. As John Gardner has observed:

When our nation was founded, there was a holy Roman Emperor, Venice was a Republic, France was ruled by a King, China and Japan by an Emperor, Russia by a Czar and Great Britain had only the barest beginnings of a democracy. All of these proud regimes and scores of others have long since passed into history, and among the world's powers, the only government that stands essentially unchanged is the Federal Union put together in the 1780's by 13 states on the east coast of North America.

Preserving and enhancing this Union is our most important goal. And in doing so, reopening the communication between our Presidents and the people should be the first task in restoring responsible government. To do this, we must first arrive at a working concept of the Presidency which is strong, yet legal; capable of leading, but without dictating. We have reaped the bitter harvest of a fundamental failure in the accountability of our Presidency; now we must rebuild that accountability to ensure the success of our government.

Index

280

executive privilege doctrine, 79, 104, 117-18, 135, 183-84

fairness doctrine, 56, 209
Family Assistance Plan, 82
Farmers' Home Administration (FHA), 110-11
FBI, 11, 72, 172, 173-74, 189, 226; oversight of, 145, 153-54
Federal Communications Commission (FCC), 56-58, 202, 203, 206-7, 210
Federal Election Campaign Act (1974), 46-48, 59, 128-29, 193, 239-40, 247-48, 250-51
Federal Election Commission, 59, 193
filibuster rule, 127-30, 156-57
Finch, Robert, 83
Fisher, Louis, 109
Florida state primary, 42
Ford, Gerald, 9, 34, 53-54, 68, 88, 97, 227, 241; and media, 210-11; and Nixon pardon, 19, 187-88; and succession, 74-75; and War Powers Act, 137
foreign affairs, as effect on Presidential ascendancy, 8-11, 13, 83-84, 106, 111-15, 122-24, 177-78
Fraser, Donald, 250-51
Freedom of Information Act, 147, 148, 226-27
Fritchey, Clayton, 179

Gardner, John, 61, 277
Goldwater, Barry, 34, 35, 57, 235
Graham, Billy, 173
Grant, Ulysses S., 108
Gray, L. Patrick, III, 116
Gulf of Tonkin resolution, 14, 112-13

Haldeman, H. R., 173-74
Hamilton, Alexander, 111, 115, 166, 179, 180, 195
Hand, Learned, 263
Harding, Warren G., 35, 219
Harriman, Averell, 242
Haynesworth, Clement, 116
Helms, Richard, 175
Hickel, Walter, 116
Hoover, Herbert, 86
Hoover, J. Edgar, 174, 175

House Judiciary Committee Impeachment proceedings, 117, 168-69, 174, 181, 185, 190, 213, 215, 237
Humphrey, Hubert, 34, 260
Hunt, Howard, 175
Huston plan, 175
Hyman, Sidney, 221

impeachment: as executive restraint, 107, 166-71, 181; "indictable crime" theory of, 167-68, 181; of Johnson, 167-68, 170-71; of Nixon, 179-90
impoundment of funds, 12, 107-11, 131-32, 135, 139, 140-42; court cases on, 146-47
intelligence programs, oversight of, 118-19
International Civil Aviation, 114
investigation power of Congress, as executive restraint, 79, 83-84, 97-98, 100, 116-17, 143-46, 152-54
IRS, 11, 172, 173, 189, 226
item veto, 108-9

Jackson, Andrew, 199
Jackson, Robert H., 9, 177
Jefferson, Thomas, 8, 67, 108, 112, 146, 198
Johnson, Andrew, impeachment of, 167-68, 170-71
Johnson, Lyndon, 73, 117, 242-43; foreign policy of, 10, 13-14, 16-17; and media, 198, 203, 208; 1964 election, 57, 235
judicial branch, as restraint on executive, 146-47, 176-78, 183-84
Justice Department, 11, 72, 172, 189; as agency of President, 190-92

Kalmbach, Herbert, 40
Kefauver, Estes, 148
Kennedy, John F., 85, 99, 117, 238, 254; assassination of, 68, 73; and media, 198, 203, 208, 219, 221-22; 1960 election, 28-29, 267
Kissinger, Henry, 83, 84, 89, 102, 240
Knox, Henry, 257
Korematsu case, 9
Krim, Arthur, 242

281